Dear reader,
I pray that you will grow in your walk with God and dig into His Word even more as a result of reading this devotional. He loves you unconditionally. Keep that in mind as you see what living an abundant Christian life looks like.
Stay in the Word, stay close to the Shepherd, and let Him lead you in paths of righteousness.
With Hope in His Service,

Heather Helmering

All Scriptures are from the King James Version.

Day One

Are You Living Abundantly?

No one hopes their future will be tedious, full of trials, heartache, or sorrow. You may desire to inspire others and possibly have some degree of success while surrounded by family and friends. It is easy to focus on and hope for the best when envisioning your future.

If you ask a child what they want to be when they grow up, they usually have very ambitious goals because, to them, anything is possible. But somewhere along the way, that child-like faith and joy gets lost.

So, is it possible to live abundantly? Is this kind of life possible for everyone? Is there a secret recipe somewhere?

Yes, yes, and no are the simple answers to your questions.

What exactly does it even mean to live abundantly?

The dictionary defines it this way: "in large quantities; plentifully." Some synonyms include: extremely, significantly, decidedly, and extensively.

To live abundantly, you must first have a goal, a purpose. What is yours? Maybe you want to raise your family in church and your children to grow up loving and serving the Lord with their lives. You may be newly married and just trying to figure out this new phase in life. Are you a college student trying to navigate the responsibilities and trials this season brings? Wherever you are in life, you have something you are working towards, hoping for, and praying for.

Next, you have steps you are taking to reach that goal. If you are a mama trying to raise her babies for the honor and glory of God, your steps are different than those of a college student. Do not compare your path to that of someone else's. They aren't going to the same place you are, and that's okay.

You must decide what is important to you. Are your dreams and goals all that matter? What about relationships along the way? You affect those around you, whether you wish to or not. What kind of impact are you making on others?

Jesus said in John 10:10, "The thief cometh not, but for to steal, and to kill, and to destroy: I am come that they may have life, and that they may have it more abundantly." This verse applies to you, friend. Through Christ, you are able to experience that abundant life!

You must live every day with purpose. Let Jesus be that purpose in your heart and life. Follow His leading and His plan for you. Let all that you do, be done to honor and please Jesus. He loves you

unconditionally and wants nothing but what is right
and good for your life.

This takes choosing to faithfully and
intentionally serve Jesus every day. Determine to fill
your heart and life with His Word. Isaiah 26:3 says,
"Thou wilt keep him in perfect peace, whose mind is
stayed on thee: because he trusteth in thee." Did you
catch that? Perfect peace. Who couldn't use more of
that?

Only you can decide how you will live. You will
have trials, heartache, and sorrow, but you don't have
to go through them alone, and you can have peace
rather than turmoil and chaos. Philippians 4:7 "And
the peace of God which passeth all understanding,
shall keep your hearts and minds through Christ
Jesus." It's all in Him.

Dear Jesus,
Please help me to focus on You and Your will for my
life. Help me trust You as You lead me into the
abundant life You have for me. Thank You for loving
me and knowing what is best for me.
In Christ's name,
Amen.

Day Two

How to Begin Living Abundantly

It starts with Jesus.

You can live your entire life with purpose and intention and meet big goals. Are those goals eternal or temporal? What becomes of your purpose and intent when you die? James 5:14 says, "Whereas ye know not what shall be on the morrow. For what is your life? It is even a vapour, that appeareth for a little time, and then vanisheth away." This truth should motivate you to make the most of each day. You will have that small dash on your obituary and headstone one day. What will the dash represent?

There is nothing wrong with being in business, having goals, and receiving promotions. But is this all you are living for? You should diligently do whatever God has called you to, but there is more to life than that job. Your company will have a posting to replace you within hours of your death. They will continue without you. That job is temporary.

Likewise, there is nothing wrong with being a stay-at-home wife and mom. It is one of the best jobs and privileges in the world! Your days are full of errands, cooking, dishes, laundry, baths, and bedtime stories. But is this all you are living for? Are you simply getting the chores done and everyone in bed on time to do it again the next day? I hope you want your life to count for something greater than that.

So, how do you get there? It begins with salvation. Salvation is a free gift that is offered and available to everyone. God says in 2 Peter 3:9, "The Lord is not slack concerning his promise, as some men count slackness; but is longsuffering to us-ward, not willing that any should perish, but that all should come to repentance." You have the choice to reject or receive this gift. No one can force you to take it or do it for you.

Why is it free? Because the Creator of the Universe, God, loves you. Right where you are, He loves you. Before you were born, He loved you. God clearly says this in John 3:16. "For God so loved the world, that he gave his only begotten Son, that whosoever believeth in him should not perish, but have everlasting life." God's unchanging and unconditional love is the love you need to place your confidence in and share with others— love that gives above and beyond anything you could earn or ever deserve.

A little over two thousand years ago, a virgin girl named Mary gave birth to a very special Baby Boy. The Baby would be no ordinary Child- He was

God, but He was also human at the same time. Many times, hundreds of years earlier, this news was foretold. Many prophets prophesied that this would happen. When the angel came to Mary, he also told her that the Child's name would be Jesus because He would save people from their sins. Jesus was born and raised under the care of Mary and her husband, Joseph.

Throughout His whole life, Jesus was perfect. Jesus living a sinless life is vital to the salvation that God offers. He is the only Person ever born that was perfect. No one will ever live a perfect life. Every human is born with a sinful nature. No one has to teach you to lie, cheat, or be mean. Because of this sinful nature, you have naturally rebelled against God's laws and standards.

God says He must judge sin, and the sinner must pay the debt of sin. If you live your entire life in separation from God, you will die in the same condition, spending eternity in complete separation from Him in a place of torment called Hell. But you have a choice. You can accept this gift and spend eternity in Heaven when you die, or you can reject it and spend eternity in Hell.

Since Jesus is perfect, He is the only One who could rightfully die to pay your sin debt. Accepting salvation means you don't have to pay eternal punishment for your sin. He died on a cross one Friday afternoon. But the story wasn't over! A follower of Jesus had gone to the tomb Sunday morning, and to her surprise, it was empty! Jesus was alive! Jesus had defeated sin, death, and the devil.

Accepting salvation is how you begin to live abundantly. You must come to the place of realizing that you are a sinner and that you have broken God's law. Romans 10:13 promises, "For whosoever shall call upon the name of the Lord shall be saved." Believing this truth takes faith.

If you are ready to take this step of faith and start living your life with a new sense of direction and purpose, all you have to do is take a moment right where you are and pray. The words in this prayer aren't magical or supernatural. I will give you a sample prayer you can use, but ultimately, you must believe in your heart that Jesus paid for your sins and that without accepting His salvation, you will spend eternity in torment and separation from God.

"Lord, I know that I am a sinner. If I died today, I would not go to heaven. Forgive my sin, come into my heart, and be my personal Lord and Saviour. I am trusting You to take my soul to Heaven when I die. Help me live for You from this day forward. In Jesus' name, Amen."

If you believe in your heart that this is true and have prayed and asked God to save you, then you are saved. Forever. Nothing past, present, or future can change this. Ephesians 1:13-14 "In whom ye also trusted, after that ye heard the word of truth, the gospel of your salvation: in whom also after that ye believed, ye were sealed with that holy Spirit of promise, Which is the earnest of our inheritance until the redemption of the purchased possession, unto the praise of his glory."

Salvation is the first step in living abundantly. Jesus said in John 10:10, "The thief cometh not, but for to steal, and to kill, and to destroy: I am come that they might have life, and that they might have it more abundantly." Jesus desires for you to experience abundant life. Living for the Lord is how you live abundantly in the mundane days of being an employee, friend, spouse, and parent. When you walk with Jesus, you see Him fulfill your life as nothing else can.

Dear Jesus,
Thank You for loving me enough to die for me. I am so thankful to be Your child. Please help me always to be grateful for my salvation. Lord, I ask that You lead me to live my life in a way that honors You as I seek You each day. Thank You for making this abundant life available to me.
In the saving name of Jesus,
Amen.

Before going to day 3, I want to emphasize an essential truth. Living abundantly is made possible by Jesus. Without salvation, we can't begin this journey. Please do not take this as adding works to salvation. Salvation is by faith alone in Christ alone, and that's it. The concepts I have shared in this book are not legalism. This study will help you live how Christ calls you to so you can experience His blessings, joy, and peace. Just as you must eat to survive, you must accept salvation to begin living abundantly. As with food, you can eat healthy foods or choose junk food. Junk food will not nourish and strengthen you. You'll survive but not thrive. This principle is the same for the truths we will begin studying. They will help you thrive as you feast on God's Word rather than live a weak and malnourished Christian life. I hope this explanation brings clarity rather than confusion.

Day Three

Living Abundantly Through Standards

Standard: principles of conduct informed by notions of honor and decency.

Where do you get your standards for living? We all have different standards. You can't, and shouldn't, always compare your standards to those of someone else. It is okay to learn from others, but you shouldn't use other imperfect humans as the final authority in your life.

Some get their standards from society. If something is socially acceptable, they allow it to be a satisfactory standard in their life. Others may look to authority. For example, they may say what is legally permissible is a good standard of living. For some, that authority may be parents, meaning their standards are merely tradition. Have you ever thought, "Well, I'm not sure; we've just always done it that way"? And some find their standards in the Bible.

You have learned how to begin this abundant life Jesus talks about in John 10:10. Now, you will learn how to practically live abundantly in the midst of life.

Salvation is just the beginning! Jesus wants you to have an abundant life every day.

Think of an area or two where you have standards such as dress, the company you allow yourself or your children to keep, entertainment you participate in, your language, how you keep your home, etc. You fill in whatever blank(s) that fit your life.

Do you remember being a child and hearing grown-ups say, "Because I said so," and that was why you had to do something? I sure do. I hated that response. I wanted to thoroughly understand the purpose of what I was doing. That has not changed much now that I am an adult with children. Maybe you can relate.

In our home, we try to keep the Bible as our standard. While we are not perfect, we trust and believe God is. That belief comes from the Bible and the examples we have witnessed in the lives of others. I firmly know and believe that we can trust the Lord unconditionally.

Although I am a Christian, that does not mean I have all the answers. But that does not change my beliefs and standards. Since I do not have all the answers, there are still times God leads a certain way or does not answer a prayer in the way I had hoped He would, and I do not understand why. But I do have a few things I do know. I know I have the Bible and its promises. I know God loves me (John 3:16). I know He will never leave me (Hebrews 13:5). I know He sees things that I do not (Isaiah 55:8-9). I know He leads in the best direction for me (Proverbs 3:5-7). Trusting God based on these truths is comforting and makes it easier to accept His will when I don't understand His plans.

The best part of this? The Bible never changes! God never changes! Hebrews 11:38 reassures us, "Jesus Christ the same yesterday, and to day, and for ever."

These truths are for you, too! You have something constant, regardless of what is happening in your life or this world! He is still working. His Word is still applicable in today's world. That is why it is essential to know the Bible. Read it daily and seek to learn more about God and His plan for you. He desires a personal relationship with you. Knowing Scripture and knowing God is not just for pastors and evangelists!

Fellowshipping with other believers is also vital to your Christian walk. You get to see God working in the lives of others, strengthening your faith. Seeing as God knows everything, He never changes, and He loves you, you have grounds enough to trust Him and His leading in your life.

If your standards come from society, why? Society is ever-changing and changing quickly. Why wouldn't you want something steady in your life? Something stable when your world is shaking? A light in the darkest night? That stability will not come from the world and its temporary comforts.

I don't know what trials and changes you may face. But I do know Who has the answers, has peace that passes all understanding, understands even though no one else does, and is always ready to listen to your burdens and carry them for you. I do know the One Who sees every tear. First Peter 5:7 says, "Casting all your care upon him; for he careth for you." Philippians 4:7 says, "And the peace of God, which passeth all understanding, shall keep your hearts and minds through Christ Jesus."

He has given standards of living for your benefit. Living within these boundaries brings protection. When driving on a curvy mountain road, you aren't mad that the guardrail is there to keep you from plummeting off the side of the mountain. God's Word and the standards within are like that guardrail. They keep you in His will, in safety, and out of sin and heartache. The Bible is the sturdy foundation you are searching for, not only for you but for your children and those you influence.

You will find peace, comfort, balance, and blessings you have never imagined and cannot begin to understand until you start living your life based on the Bible's standards. Isaiah 26:3 says, "Thou wilt keep him in perfect peace, whose mind is stayed on thee: because he trusteth in thee." Second Corinthians 1:3, "Blessed be God, even the Father of our Lord Jesus Christ, the Father of mercies, and the God of all comfort;"

It is okay if you are reading this and aren't sure about the Bible. You may be skeptical if it all really works. After all, society says it's just a fairy tale that some people use as a crutch to get through life. If that is where you are, that's fine. I understand. I would like to leave you with this thought: What if there is some validity to this? What if this is the thing you are looking for? What is the worst thing that could happen if you try it? Walking with Christ, trusting Him, and His will for your life will lead to an abundant life, unlike anything in this world.

Father,
Thank You for giving us Your Word and the principles to live by. I may not always understand or agree, but help me to remember that living by Your principles brings peace and joy that we can't experience apart from You. I want to trust that Your standards and boundaries are for my good and protection. Thank You for loving me enough to give me guidelines protecting my life and testimony.
In the name of Jesus,
Amen.

Day Four

Living Abundantly Through Forgiveness

"And be ye kind one to another, tenderhearted, forgiving one another, even as God for Christ's sake hath forgiven you." Ephesians 4:32

We all like to receive forgiveness but don't always find giving it easy.

However, it is a command. God does not desire anyone to live with an unforgiving spirit. Unforgiveness leads to bitterness and is destructive. Hebrews 12:15 says bitterness is a root. Once it begins to grow, it spreads quickly. "Looking diligently lest any man fail of the grace of God; lest any root of bitterness springing up trouble you, and thereby many be defiled;" The bitterness in your heart will cloud your view of people and situations, and your walk with God will be affected. You cannot live the abundant life when you are filled with unforgiveness and bitterness.

Christ has forgiven you of so much! It is up to you to forgive as you have been forgiven. Colossians 3:13 says, "Forbearing one another, and forgiving one another, if any man have a quarrel against any: even as Christ forgave you, so also do ye." Mark 11:25 says, "And when ye stand praying, forgive, if ye have ought against any: that your Father also which is in heaven may forgive you your trespasses." God does not owe you anything. He chooses to forgive when you ask, and you are to offer forgiveness as freely as Christ. He does not make you earn it or pray a certain amount of times before being forgiven. First John 1:9 is a promise that says, "If we confess our sins, he is faithful and just to forgive us our sins, and to cleanse us from all unrighteousness."

Unforgiveness is like a prison. There's no peace or joy there. You will not serve the Lord until you deal with it. Thankfully, it is easy to get out of this prison. You have the key! You must go to the person you are struggling to forgive, kindly ask if you can speak to them, tell them how you feel, what caused this, and forgive them. Do not wait for someone to ask for this forgiveness. They may not even know they did anything to upset you; therefore, the request will never come.

Additionally, your prayer life will be hindered when you have unforgiveness in your heart. When you have a problem between yourself and another person, God wants you to get that right before praying to Him. We must get right with others and then get things right with God. "Therefore if thou bring thy gift to the altar, and there rememberest that thy brother hath ought against thee; Leave there thy gift before the altar, and go thy way; first be reconciled to thy brother, and then come and offer thy gift." Matthew 5:23-24

It is easy to stay mad, withhold forgiveness, and justify your attitude and actions when you are hurt. But that is not where God wants you to stay. Trust Him. Choose to live in obedience and have a forgiving spirit so you can live abundantly as Jesus desires.

Dear Heavenly Father,
Thank You for the forgiveness You have shown me.
Thank You for Calvary and for forgiving me every day.
I desire to live freely and abundantly. I do not want to live in bondage to unforgiveness and bitterness.
Thank You for showing me how important forgiveness is! Forgive me for the bitterness and unforgiveness I have held on to. Please help me to forgive others as I have been forgiven.
In the forgiving name of Christ,
Amen.

Day Five

Living Abundantly Through Compassion

Compassion is defined as sympathetic pity and concern for the sufferings or misfortunes of others. Jude verse 22 says, "And of some have compassion, making a difference:" That is the power of compassion! Too often, the world says that you should only care for and help those that care for and help you or treat others how they treat you. I want to remind you that that advice is not Bible!

The origin is Latin: compati: to suffer with. Where we also get our word compatible. Having compassion requires purpose and intention. You must look around you and take notice of others. This also means giving the benefit of the doubt. Compassion pushes you out of your comfort zone. It forces you to see people and look beyond the outward appearances and the initial, sinful judgments and opinions you may have about them. Christians tend to forget that lost people look and act like lost people. Do not use that as an excuse to ignore them; instead, use it as motivation to show them Jesus. You are already going to Heaven; what do you have to lose? Time? Energy? That is NOTHING compared to that person spending eternity in Hell!

Matthew 9:36, "But when he saw the multitudes, he was moved with compassion on them, because they fainted, and were scattered abroad, as sheep having no shepherd." Friend, that is us! We are compared to sheep over and over again. We need the Shepherd!

Jude 1:22, "And of some have compassion, making a difference." This will be how some people come to Christ, not through fear of Hell and death, but by seeing Christlike compassion in your life, testimony, and behavior toward people- the saved and the lost.

You have probably been hurt by words at some point. You might have been wounded by the words of others, even if that wasn't their intent. It can be hard to move past whether it was an accident or an intentional offense. You don't seek to be hurt by others. Hurt people hurt people. You don't know what someone is going through. Your happiest friends are possibly battling depression. You just NEVER know.

This is why it is vital to be Christlike and show compassion to others when given the opportunity, even when you have been hurt.

Think of the opposite of this. How is your day or mood impacted when you receive a compliment, a word of encouragement, a small gift, help to complete a task, or know someone is praying for you? Simple acts of compassion can make a huge difference. Be the one to make that difference for someone else today.

Compassion is **action**. If there's no action, all you have is sympathy. Compassion is *selfless*, takes *purpose*, and takes *time.* Showing compassion is not always convenient or comfortable, but it is ALWAYS worth it.

Showing compassion doesn't mean you agree with every aspect of that person's life. Just because they look different from you doesn't mean they don't need encouragement. Just because they go to a different church or use a different Bible doesn't mean they don't need to be encouraged by another child of God. Your fellow Christian brothers and sisters are not exempt from needing compassion! Bear ye one another's burdens and so fulfill the law of Christ. Compassionate is what God calls us to be! We do not know the battles others are silently fighting.

The next time you are out, and you see a mom struggling to manage her toddler's temper tantrum while looking for her screaming infant's pacifier, ask if she would like a hand rather than silently judging her. Maybe you assume the toddler is spoiled or she's a single mom. Neither of which concerns you or changes the fact that you have the ability to show compassion to her for just a minute of her challenging day. Christ never said only to be compassionate to those with well-behaved children.

While you are out shopping, taking care of errands, or on the phone on hold for the third time, try to be compassionate. Give them the benefit of the doubt. What if that cashier wasn't trying to be inattentive and that phone representative wasn't trying to be hateful? What if they just received a phone call of bad news right before they had to speak to you?

Be the reason someone smiles, even just for a moment. It takes more time to judge someone and decide whether they deserve compassion than it does just to be compassionate. Showing compassion is how we experience joy and abundant living. By caring about what Jesus cares about. People.

Dear Jesus,
Thank You for the compassion You have for me. Without compassion, there would have been no Calvary, forgiveness, and salvation. I would be lost and on my way to Hell. Thank You for showing compassion and allowing me to see my need for You. Thank you for walking with me daily and consistently showing me compassion. Help me to show that same compassion to others. Sometimes I am quick to judge or look the other way, but that is not what You would do. Often, those closest to me get even less compassion from me. Forgive me for being selfish and not seeing the needs of others.
In the name of Jesus,
Amen.

Day Six

Living Abundantly Through Faith and Obedience

Have you ever tried encouraging someone by telling them to "just trust the Lord"? Has this phrase ever been said to you? It can be a comfort, and sometimes we must be reminded to focus on God and His plan, especially during a trial.

But what does it *really* mean to trust the Lord? Trust is "a firm belief in the reliability, truth, ability, or strength of someone or something." You can't have confidence in something you haven't tested; otherwise, you don't know if it is trustworthy. The Bible commands you to trust the Lord.

Psalm 115:11 "Ye that fear the LORD, trust in the LORD: he is their help and their shield." He is a help and shield to those who fear and trust Him. He doesn't give this promise to everyone.

Isaiah 26:4 "Trust ye in the LORD for ever: for in the LORD JEHOVAH is everlasting strength:"

Psalm 4:5 "Offer the sacrifices of righteousness, and put your trust in the LORD."

Psalm 118:8-9 "It is better to trust in the LORD than to put confidence in man. It is better to trust in the LORD than to put confidence in princes."

Proverbs 3:5 "Trust in the LORD with all thine heart; and lean not unto thine own understanding."

The other side of the trust coin is obedience. The Bible says If you love Him, you will keep His commandments. Being a Christian is more than having the "right" look and vocabulary. Anyone can quickly learn to say things like "Praise the Lord," "I'm praying for you," and" Just trust the Lord." Would you think of saying, "I don't love God enough to obey Him"? He knows your heart regardless of what comes out of your mouth.

His Word gives promises for obedience. Others can tell stories of what happened when they obeyed. Trust and obedience are two sides of the same coin.

Will you live in obedience to the Lord?

"And Samuel said, Hath the LORD as great delight in burnt offerings and sacrifices, as in obeying the voice of the LORD? Behold, to obey is better than sacrifice, and to hearken than the fat of rams." 1 Samuel 15:22.

Dear Jesus,
It is easy to say that I trust You, but it is not always easy to put that into practice through obedience. My flesh faces fear and doubt. I am thankful You already know this. Lord, I am asking You to help me overcome those fears and doubts and turn them into faith and obedience. I want to be an obedient Christian. I know there are blessings and joy that only come when I live how You have commanded in Your Word. Thank You for giving me free will, but I want to use that free will to live my life for You.
In the name of Jesus,
Amen.

Day Seven

Living Abundantly Through Purity

We often hear the importance of mental and physical purity being taught to children. While I agree, we must also remember that many of the same principles apply to adults.

Some of the most common things we hope to teach our children are things like abstaining from drugs and alcohol, saving sex for marriage, and overall being kind and respectful humans. Did you know that all of these are Biblical principles? Each principle should also apply to you. God's principles aren't only for those under 18 or those living at home or on a college campus. God wants you to use His Word as your standard of living because that is the path to an abundant life.

God gives many practical and necessary guides for daily living on Its pages. You will never outgrow God. It doesn't matter how long you have been saved; you will never become a grown-up Christian who leaves home. Praise God for that! You get to live each day with our Lord beside you, guiding and helping you.

As a married person, do you take care to keep yourself pure? Do you stay faithful to your wedding vows? Are you vigilant about resisting the snares of the devil? If you have not learned this yet, Satan is out to destroy your marriage by any means necessary. Purity still applies to you even when you are married. You are still responsible for keeping your heart and mind right and your body pure within the marriage relationship.

If you are single, are you remaining pure while you wait for God's will for your life? Are you choosing friends that encourage this purity? You must remember God's principles for pure living. Keep your focus on Him.

Christian, God has commanded you to be an example to others. You can only be an example once you are first obedient. 1 Timothy 4:12 says, "Let no man despise thy youth; but be thou an example of the believers, in word, in conversation, in charity, in spirit, in faith, in purity."

You are not to have the works of the flesh reigning in your life. I love the wording and reminder Paul gives us in Colossians 3:1-10. "If ye then be risen with Christ, seek those things which are above, where Christ sitteth on the right hand of God. Set your affection on things above, not on things on the earth. For ye are dead, and your life is hid with Christ in God. When Christ, who is our life, shall appear, then shall ye also appear with him in glory. Mortify therefore your members which are upon the earth; fornication, uncleanness, inordinate affection, evil concupiscence, and covetousness, which is idolatry: For which things' sake the wrath of God cometh on the children of disobedience: In the which ye also walked some time, when ye lived in them. But now ye also put off all these; anger, wrath, malice, blasphemy, filthy communication out of your mouth. Lie not one to another, seeing that ye have put off the old man with his deeds; And have put on the new man, which is renewed in knowledge after the image of him that created him;"

Ephesians 5:1-4 says, "Be ye therefore followers of God, as dear children; And walk in love, as Christ also hath loved us, and hath given himself for us an offering and a sacrifice to God for a sweetsmelling savour. But fornication, and all uncleanness, or covetousness, let it not be once named among you, as becometh saints; Neither filthiness, nor foolish talking, nor jesting, which are not convenient: but rather giving of thanks."

Romans 12:1 "I beseech you therefore, brethren, by the mercies of God, that ye present your bodies a living sacrifice, holy, acceptable unto God, which is your reasonable service."

Hebrews 12:1 "Wherefore seeing we also are compassed about with so great a cloud of witnesses, let us lay aside every weight, and the sin which doth so easily beset us, and let us run with patience the race that is set before us,"

1 Corinthians 6:18 "Flee fornication. Every sin that a man doeth is without the body; but he that committeth fornication sinneth against his own body."

Psalm 101:3 "I will set no wicked thing before mine eyes: I hate the work of them that turn aside; it shall not cleave to me."

1 Thessalonians 5:22 "Abstain from all appearance of evil."

1 Peter 1:15-16 "But as he which hath called you is holy, so be ye holy in all manner of conversation; Because it is written, Be ye holy; for I am holy."

Galatians 5:19-23 "Now the works of the flesh are manifest, which are these; Adultery, fornication, uncleanness, lasciviousness, Idolatry, witchcraft, hatred, variance, emulations, wrath, strife, seditions, heresies, Envyings, murders, drunkenness, revellings, and such like: of the which I tell you before, as I have also told you in time past, that they which do such things shall not inherit the kingdom of God. But the fruit of the Spirit is love, joy, peace, longsuffering, gentleness, goodness, faith, Meekness, temperance: against such there is no law."

Leviticus 20:7 "Sanctify yourselves therefore, and be ye holy: for I am the Lord your God."

It is apparent what the Lord expects. You should use your body to serve the Lord, not fulfill the lusts of the world and the flesh. Your body and life are not your own. Be assured that there are consequences for living in sin. First Corinthians 6:20 "For ye are bought with a price: therefore glorify God in your body, and in your spirit, which are God's." God always wants what is best for you. He does not give boundaries to make you miserable; instead, He gives you freedom. Living in sin is bondage. The devil is a liar and will never show the result of your choices. God has given you free will, but you cannot choose the consequences of your actions. If you decide to live in obedience to God's Word, your life will have more joy and peace. When you live a pure life, you will experience the abundant Christian life God has for you. You will know Him deeper when you trust Him and live by His principles. I hope you are seeking to know Jesus deeper every day.

Dear Jesus,
Thank you for giving me guidelines for purity. The world looks down on this lifestyle, and sometimes, I feel alone. Thank You for the reminder that You are always with me and choosing purity is always worth it. Father, I ask that You help me live a pure life. Thank You for Your love for me.
In the name of Jesus,
Amen.

Day Eight

Living Abundantly Through
Delighting in His Word

Reading God's Word can be viewed as a chore or burden. You may treat it as something you must do as if it is a spiritual obligation or expectation. It takes time and effort to read, study, and memorize Scripture. Devotions can seem even more challenging when you have children in the home. Your flesh will not encourage you to read the Bible, either. Letting everything else on your to-do list precede your quiet time with the Lord is easy. It is vital to regularly make time to get alone with, hear from, and fellowship with God.

Do not compare your quiet time with someone else's. I am a homeschool mom and a night owl, so I am not up at 4 A.M. to have my devotions. If you do, that's great! Thankfully God is always available, so be faithful to get alone with Him daily.

When you take the time to get into His Word, He meets you there. Jesus wants you to find delight in His Word and His presence. He also delights in this time with you. Jesus Christ and the Word are the same. John 1:1-2 teaches, "In the beginning was the Word, and the Word was with God, and the Word was God. The same was in the beginning with God." Do not write off reading your Bible as just something to do. You are spending time with God the Father!

Psalm 1:1-2 says, "Blessed is the man that walketh not in the counsel of the ungodly, nor standeth in the way of sinners, nor sitteth in the seat of the scornful. But his delight is in the law of the LORD; and in his law doth he meditate day and night."

Psalm 119:47 says, "And I will delight myself in thy commandments, which I have loved."

Psalm 119:16 says, "I will delight myself in thy statutes: I will not forget thy word."

God has written and preserved His Word for you. He reveals Himself to you through His written Word. He wants you to know Him! When you take the time to get in His Word, you will know Him and delight in His presence. The opposite is also true. When you neglect His Word, you fill up on the things of the world, and experience more despair than delight.

In His Word you find delight, joy, comfort, strength, and the abundant life you desire. Take the time to dig into the Bible and know Jesus for yourself. Jesus understands what you're going through, and His Word is sufficient.

Dear Jesus,
Thank You for Your Word. Thank You for preserving it and writing it for me. I am thankful I can read it and live according to Your principles freely. I am so glad You care about the details of my life. You have provided a way for me to know and experience You. Thank You for showing me how to live the victorious, abundant Christian life.
In the name of Jesus,
Amen.

Day Nine

Living Abundantly Through Grace

Grace is one of those things that just amazes me. Grace is something most of us want to receive. We know how precious it is, yet, we want to offer it less than we would like to receive it. Have we forgotten that it is by grace that we are saved, able to fellowship with God, have wisdom, and one day enjoy the sights of Heaven? Ephesians 2:8 assures us, "For by grace ye are saved through faith; and that not of yourselves: it is the gift of God:"

God is not stingy with grace; you should not be, either. The grace you receive and give comes from Him, and He has an abundant supply! Hebrews 4:16 says, "Let us therefore come boldly unto the throne of grace, that we may obtain mercy, and find grace to help in time of need." God is inviting you into His presence! Webster's 1828 Dictionary defines grace as 1) "Favor; good will; kindness; disposition to oblige another;" 2) Appropriately, the free unmerited love of God, the spring and source of all benefits men receive from Him." That is powerful!

God bestows His love, favor, kindness, and goodwill on His children because He is God. Psalm 68:19 says, "Blessed be the Lord, who daily loadeth us with benefits, even the God of our salvation. Selah."

Regardless of where you are and how bad things are going, you are still experiencing God's grace and benefits.

Why is it difficult to show this grace to other people? One reason is forgetting the true Source of grace. You do not have to decide if another person is worthy of experiencing grace from you. They probably aren't. But you also do not deserve the grace you have from God either. Show grace to others because of the grace you have received. His grace is perfect, sufficient, strengthening, freeing, and protective. You would not want to see where your life would be were it not for the grace of God.

Realizing how blessed you are, how good God is, the miracles you have experienced, the prayers you have seen answered, and the wisdom you have access to, it should lead you to tell others about Jesus so they can experience Him, too. He has enough grace for everyone. Sharing the Source of grace with others and extending grace leads to an abundant Christian life.

Second Corinthians 12:9, "And he said unto me, My grace is sufficient for thee: for my strength is made perfect in weakness. Most gladly therefore will I rather glory in my infirmities, that the power of Christ may rest upon me." You can trust God in any situation. His grace is sufficient!

James 4:6, "But he giveth more grace. Wherefore he saith, God resisteth the proud, but giveth grace unto the humble." God wants to extend grace to everyone, but a heart full of pride is not a place God can work.

First Corinthians 15:10, "But by the grace of God I am what I am: and his grace which was bestowed upon me was not in vain; but I laboured more abundantly than they all: yet not I, but the grace of God which was with me." The apostle Paul knew what the grace of God had done for him. All that he seemingly accomplished for the Lord was just the Lord working through him. Paul lived in obedience because of the grace he experienced. God significantly used Paul, and he is an excellent example of living an abundant life through obedience and grace.

Dear Jesus,
Thank You for this grace. I do not know where I would be had You not shown grace to me. I am thankful that Your grace does not run out and that I do not have to seek to earn it. Thank You for loving me and freely giving grace to me. Help me, Father, to extend that grace to others. Not only to be kind and meet physical needs but to bring them to You, the true Source of grace.
In the name of Jesus,
Amen.

Day Ten

Living Abundantly Through Prayer

Have you ever heard someone speak about a significant or specific prayer that they witnessed God answer? Such as a missionary with a powerful account of God's protection or a seasoned saint recounting a revival service where the power of God was present, and dozens got saved. Perhaps you have heard your grandparents tell you things they have seen God do. You can read biographies of previous generations, such as A.W.Tozer, Jim Elliot, and Hudson Taylor. People with great faith were sold out for Jesus and saw big things happen.

If you read any works from the preachers of yesteryear, you will find a common thread: prayer. These accounts get treated as fictional stories instead of literal accounts of the power of the Living God. Have you heard an account like that and thought God just doesn't do that anymore? Have you forgotten that God never changes?

Where is your faith? Unbelief is partially due to spiritual laziness. Seeing God do great things takes work. It takes faith and prayer. You will only get miraculous experiences with the work of prayer. Faith and prayer are not easy, nor do they come naturally.

Jesus Himself prayed to the Father and also reminds you to pray. If He felt the need to pray, how much more do you need to! You see, prayer brings you into the presence of God. Prayer humbles and reminds you of your need for God's leading and intervention because you can't do this alone. Prayer gets you still and quiet to hear God speak. He wants to align your heart with His so you learn to pray according to His will, not your own.

I have had the privilege of seeing God answer specific prayers, and you can, too!

When I was pregnant with my second child, my daughter, I knew she would be premature. My body does not carry babies very long. My first was born at twenty-six weeks. At twenty-two weeks with my daughter, I was hospitalized due to complications. During my internal pity party, God said, "Haven't I told you to pray specifically?" I answered yes and that I was. I was praying for a healthy full-term baby. Of course, I was. Of course, I KNEW God could easily let her be a full-term baby if He wanted. He replied that I was not praying specifically. He wanted me to pray for a specific week. I said forty, and God said no. I went back and forth with God until thirty-seven weeks, and He clearly said, "Thirty-five. Thirty-five weeks."

All I could say was, "Yes, Lord." I began to pray for thirty-five weeks. I had never been that pregnant before, and sitting at twenty-two weeks, that felt like an eternity away. I started having Braxton-Hicks contractions at twenty-seven weeks but knew I would not deliver before thirty-five weeks. When I was thirty-five weeks and one day, at 1 A.M., my water broke at home, which was another heart desire God answered.

Last summer, my husband had to buy a new belt for the lawnmower. That crazy thing was $75. Around this time, a stray dog was hanging around our house. We had left one day for a few hours, and the new belt was missing when we returned home. My husband and son looked around our yard and couldn't find it. It was dark, so I encouraged them to wait until morning and look again. As I tucked my teenager into bed, I prayed that we would find the belt and it would still be usable.

My husband got home from work the next day and went to the neighbor's house to see if they'd be okay with him looking in their backyard for this belt. They didn't mind at all. So my son took off through their yard and found the belt. **Unharmed.** My son saw God answer a prayer for something as simple as a lawnmower belt.

I love "big prayers." God can do exceedingly abundantly above all we could ask or think (Ephesians 3:20). He gave me Ephesians 3:20 in November of 2020 when he led me to a position at our church. This job meant leaving my long-time position as a stay-at-home, homeschool mom. At this time, we had been homeschooling for six years, and my youngest had never attended regular school. I talked with the leaders of the ministry I felt called to and was offered the job. I knew this was what God wanted. However, it was mid-November. I would start work in January, and my kids would start school at the academy at the church. We had no uniforms, backpacks, lunch boxes, water bottles, or extra money for the registration fees. Plus, Christmas, my son's birthday, and my husband's birthday were all between when I accepted the job and school started.

I clearly remember going to the Lord during my devotions and saying that I didn't want just to bring my grocery list of needs, but it was all I had that day. There was a long list and not a lot of time. He immediately gave me Ephesians 3:20 and overwhelming peace. He was going to take care of it. And He did.

God had taken care of every single bit, and on January 4th, we were all ready for this new adventure. Too often, I fear that we have faith for the "big" things but try to handle the "little" things independently. **Friend, you must remember that nothing is too small for God! He cares about every single detail of your life!** John 15:5 reminds us, "I am the vine, ye are the branches: He that abideth in me, and I in him, the same bringeth forth much fruit: for without me ye can do nothing."

Trust God with the details. Have enough faith to ask God for the big and the small things. Have enough faith to pray.

Dear Jesus,
Thank You for being patient with me when my faith isn't what it should be when I go to others before going to You. Thank You for giving me opportunities to see You move and causing my faith to grow. Even when I don't see You, I have Your Word, which I can trust. Lord, thank You for loving me and guiding me. I am so thankful I can come to You in prayer anytime. Hearing from You and knowing You listen to me is such a comfort to my weary heart. Father, thank You for the privilege of prayer. I ask that You remind me to come to You first with every praise and prayer rather than running to others.
In the name of Jesus,
Amen.

Day Eleven

Living Abundantly Through Praise

I love focusing on the power and privilege of prayer. It thrills my heart to share stories of seeing God move in ways only He can. It encourages me to hear very specific prayers God answered. Knowing that the Creator of the universe hears your prayers is just amazing, isn't it? Seeing Him care about the minor details of your life is incredible. However, you can't just stop at prayer and amazement. You must go deeper than that. You must learn to praise God as much, if not more, than you come to Him in prayer.

Webster's 1828 dictionary defines praise as a verb transitive with these four definitions:

1) To commend; to applaud; to express approbation of personal worth or actions.
2) To extol in words or song; to magnify; to glorify on account of perfections or excellent works.
3) To express gratitude for personal favors.
4) To do honor to; to display the excellence of.

Psalm 100:4 says, "Enter into his gates with thanksgiving, and into his courts with praise: be thankful unto him, and bless his name."

Hebrews 13:15 says, "By him therefore let us offer the sacrifice of praise continually, that is, the fruit of our lips giving thanks to his name."

Psalm 150:6 is a command to praise. "Let every thing that hath breath praise the Lord. Praise ye the Lord."

In these verses, God does not give a specific time to praise Him because we should always have an attitude of praise. There is never a bad or wrong time to praise God for Who He is or what He has done. Psalms 145-150 are psalms of praise to the Lord. Sometimes you may not know what to say, or your situation looks so bleak that you can't see anything good to praise Him for. Go to these psalms. Use them to pray God's Word back to Him. These psalms show us different attributes of God, acts of God, and that praise is pleasant to Him. Since God never changes, You can always praise Him for Who He is and all He has done.

Spending time in praise focuses on the Saviour rather than the situation. Praise reminds you of the times God has answered prayer and other ways you have seen Him work. Remembering His goodness encourages and gives strength to keep praying, trusting, and not quitting on God just because things are hard.

Focusing on the Lord and praising Him for being God helps you live an abundant life. When your attention is on Him, you will find peace, comfort, joy, and the desire to tell others how good God is. Sometimes that perspective shift is all that is needed to get from defeat to victory. So many struggles happen in your mind. You must keep your mind focused on Jesus.

Isaiah 26:3 says, "Thou wilt keep him in perfect peace, whose mind is stayed on thee: because he trusteth in thee."

Dear Jesus,
Thank You for giving me Scripture that shows Who You are and the words to pray when I can't find my own. I want to live a life of praise. Father, I ask that You help me keep my mind on You and that praise would come to my lips frequently. I have so much to be thankful for, even on bad days.
In the name of Jesus,
Amen.

Some things to praise God for at any time:

His mercy	His love
His grace	His forgiveness
Salvation	Prayer
Heaven	Wisdom
Health	Provision
Family	Friends
Scripture	

Day Twelve

Living Abundantly Through Your Identity in Jesus

When someone asks who you are, you probably start with your name, profession, and accomplishments. Society emphasizes what you do, what you accomplish, how productive you are, and how much money you have. But you must remember that Jesus also greatly emphasizes your identity. Your identity was never meant to be found in your job, hobbies, finances, savings account, or sexuality. Christians should find their identity in Christ. Since He never changes (Hebrews 13:8 says, "Jesus Christ the same yesterday, to day, and for ever.), your identity doesn't either. I would say that I am a Christian, wife, mom, friend, sister, and aunt. That is who I am; it is part of my identity, but not all.

What will be left when the hobbies, jobs, and money are gone? This is who you are. Who you are and what you do aren't the same. God has declared who you are.

When you base your identity on things only meant to describe you, it can cause complete disasters in other areas. Have you ever said or thought, "I just don't know who I am anymore. I feel like I have lost myself." When things change, it can be overwhelming, and a statement like that makes sense. What about that new mom who is sleep deprived? The stay-at-home mom that hardly ever leaves the house alone? They also feel like they have lost their identity as a person. Seasons of life change, and some are just plain hard. This is why you must find your identity in the stability of Christ.

Now that we've looked at what your identity is not, let's get into what it *is*. Ephesians chapter 1 is my favorite passage for this topic. In just a few verses, God calls us blessed, chosen, born again, forgiven, loved, adopted, pleasing to God, and redeemed. These things never change because they come from Scripture. Standing on these truths is how you live the abundant Christian life.

When you continue to base who you are on what you do, you live in bondage, always trying to be what others say you should be. Living this way leaves you chasing the next promotion, raise, higher degree, or spending money you do not have to keep up appearances. The opinions of others should not define you; the Lord should.

Remember that degrees and finances do not get you to Heaven or gain approval from God. Seek to know who you are in Christ, accept this as your complete identity that never changes, and begin to live the abundant life He has for you.

Dear Lord,
Thank You for making it clear in Your Word what my identity is. Thank You that You never change; regardless of what is happening in my life, I can find stability in You. Lord, I am thankful to know that my identity and salvation are secure in You. Who I am is based on Your Word, and that is enough. Please help me to trust You and live abundantly in my true identity.
In the name of Jesus,
Amen.

Day Thirteen

Living Abundantly Through Hurts

No one wants to experience pain and heartache. I don't know of anyone that is praying for trials. However, these things will come, so you must know how to walk through them while honoring the Lord and learning through the process. This is not always easy, but you can do it with Christ. God has given you the Bible to encourage and help you live abundantly during these situations. Some are much more than you could ever imagine enduring.

I have had plenty of hurts in my 30 years. I could have handled all of them better. You could probably say the same, but that does not mean you can't learn from and even appreciate the hurt you experienced. How is this possible? If you let your pain drive you to Christ rather than away from Him, extraordinary things can happen. He is the God of healing and miracles, even when you don't understand.

How do you get to this place? It starts right now. You must have a relationship with God. You won't go to someone that you don't trust. And you don't trust someone until you know them. So, you must get to know God. You will want to do that *before* the hurts come if you want to live abundantly through them. When you know and trust God, His Word will make more sense, bringing comfort and assurance that your experiences have a purpose.

For example, think of the forerunners of the Christian faith. How many people were martyrs for the faith throughout history? What if they had said no to God's call because of the dangers they faced? Look to Scripture. What if Paul had given up after the second beating or imprisonment? Remember the three Hebrew children in the Book of Daniel? There was a fourth Person in that fire with them. It was Christ! You get to see how God used their lives, how these people drew closer to God, and how He was always faithful.

The hurt you are experiencing, or will experience in the future, is real. I am not trying to downplay that. Take the pain to Jesus. I encourage everyone to have a life verse and a seasonal verse. The life verse keeps you focused on what you are trying to implement throughout your life. Mine is Proverbs 14:1. The seasonal verse is for each season. Seasons change, and the verse you're clinging to right now may not be the one you cling to next month.

When hurts come, here are a few that you can always look to for comfort.

Jeremiah 33:3, "Call unto me, and I will answer thee, and shew thee great and mighty things, which thou knowest not." You don't have to see, know, or understand why the hurt is happening. You do not have to know how God will use it later on. But you can pray, faithfully expecting an answer from your Heavenly Father, and He will show you what He wants you to know at that time. It may not be everything, and that is okay. Just remember to trust Him.

Romans 8:28, "And we know that all things work together for good to them that love God, to them who are the called according to his purpose." This is a promise. If you are a child of God, you are under His care, and all things will work together for your good. Again, you may not see that in the hurt or right after, but this is His promise.

Job 1:22 says, "In all this Job sinned not, nor charged God foolishly." If you read the account of Job and all he went through, you would agree that this was hard to do. But you will see that he had a relationship with God, and even through losing his wealth, health, and family, he chose to trust God.

Philippians 4:11-13 says, "Not that I speak in respect of want: for I have learned, in whatsoever state I am, therewith to be content. I know both how to be abased, and I know how to abound: every where and in all things I am instructed both to be full and to be hungry, both to abound and to suffer need. I can do all things through Christ which strengtheneth me." Paul said this after being beaten, shipwrecked, left for dead, and imprisoned. He was absolutely facing physical, mental, emotional, and possible spiritual hurts. But Paul trusted God. God used him significantly, and He can use you, too when you trust Him.

First Peter 5:7, "Casting all your care upon him; for he careth for you." He wants you to bring Him every hurt, need, and care. He cares about even the minor details of your life.

Matthew 10:29-31 "Are not two sparrows sold for a farthing? and one of them shall not fall on the ground without your Father. But the very hairs of your head are all numbered. Fear ye not therefore, ye are of more value than many sparrows." You may not understand why and want it to end, but you are not enduring the hurt alone. Anything a Christian faces will come only with the permission of God. He is fully aware of what is happening.

Throughout the book of Psalms, there are trials, hurts, and fear in the lives of the humans God used to pen the Scripture. And over and over, God gives the command and example to praise Him in every circumstance.

Isaiah 26:3-4, "Thou wilt keep him in perfect peace, whose mind is stayed on thee: because he trusteth in thee. Trust ye in the Lord for ever: for in the Lord Jehovah is everlasting strength:" When you focus on the Lord, praise Him, and trust Him, you can have peace in any circumstance. It doesn't make sense to have peace, joy, or comfort in the midst of hurt, but it is possible through Christ.

Second Corinthians 12:7-9 says, "And lest I should be exalted above measure through the abundance of the revelations, there was given to me a thorn in the flesh, the messenger of Satan to buffet me, lest I should be exalted above measure. For this thing I besought the Lord thrice, that it might depart from me. And he said unto me, My grace is sufficient for thee: for my strength is made perfect in weakness. Most gladly therefore will I rather glory in my infirmities, that the power of Christ may rest upon me." Paul knew why he had this thorn in the flesh. He prayed three times and asked God to remove it. The answer was no every time. May you say with Paul that you would rather have infirmities if that means the power of Christ rests upon you.

It seems more challenging to heal from hurts caused by those you love and those who are not "supposed" to hurt you. You must remember that every person is imperfect, from the pulpit to the pew. Everyone is equally sinful, needing the Holy Spirit, grace, and forgiveness. Please do not look to the pastor or deacons as the spiritually elite that should never mess up. That is unrealistic. If you have been hurt or offended by someone in the church, I beg you to take it to the Lord. Do not live in unforgiveness and bitterness.

People are not perfect, and even Christians get it wrong. Yes, Christians are to be held to a higher standard, be above reproach, and all of that. Sin is sin, and I am not excusing or justifying it.

Remember that at ANY time, it could be you needing grace and forgiveness from someone else. The Bible repeatedly says to forgive, be longsuffering, tenderhearted, kind, and loving. Even when it is hard, and you don't want to, even when you were wronged by someone that claims to love Jesus. Even then. Don't be bitter.

Hebrews 12:2a says, "Looking unto Jesus the author and finisher of our faith;" This is where our focus should be—constantly looking unto Jesus. Not the hurt and offenses we experience or the imperfections of others.

Galatians 6:1 says, "Brethren, if a man be overtaken in a fault, ye which are spiritual, restore such an one in the spirit of meekness; considering thyself, lest thou also be tempted."

Things happen, but you can choose how you will react to them. No matter what happens, He is faithful. Don't quit on Jesus because a few of His servants misrepresented Him. Choose to see the grace of God, the growth, and the lesson in the hurt. Choosing grace and forgiveness is how you grow closer to the Lord and experience the abundant Christian life in any circumstance.

Heavenly Father,
You see every aspect of my life. Thank You for the
hurts you have protected me from that I wasn't even
aware of. Thank You for the hurtful friendships and
relationships You have removed from my life. So
many things hurt at the moment, the memories hurt,
and it doesn't always make sense. I am thankful that I
can trust You and Your will for me. Hurts will come,
but Father, I pray that You will help me stay focused
on You, grow in my walk with You, and strengthen my
faith. May my hurts be part of my testimony that
glorifies You and helps others.
In the name of Jesus,
Amen.

Day Fourteen

Living Abundantly Through Prayer and Fasting

"Moreover when ye fast, be not, as the hypocrites, of a sad countenance: for they disfigure their faces, that they may appear unto men to fast. Verily I say unto you, They have their reward."
Matthew 6:16
"And when they were come to the multitude, there came to him a certain man, kneeling down to him, and saying, Lord, have mercy on my son: for he is lunatic, and sore vexed: for ofttimes he falleth into the fire, and oft into the water. And I brought him to thy disciples, and they could not cure him. Then Jesus answered and said, O faithless and perverse generation, how long shall I be with you? how long shall I suffer you? bring him hither to me. And Jesus rebuked the devil; and he departed out of him: and the child was cured from that very hour. Then came the disciples to Jesus apart, and said, Why could not we cast him out? And Jesus said unto them, Because of your unbelief: for verily I say unto you, If ye have faith as a grain of mustard seed, ye shall say unto this mountain, Remove hence to yonder place; and it shall

remove; and nothing shall be impossible unto you. Howbeit this kind goeth not out but by prayer and fasting." Matthew 17:14-21

Notice that Matthew 6 says *when,* not *if,* because Christians are expected to fast. Why? Matthew 17 shows that someone else's spiritual victory may depend on your prayer and fasting. Fasting isn't something that is usually portrayed as exciting. Giving up treats and routines doesn't come naturally. I understand that completely. Let's look at the blessings of fasting.

There are different types of fasts. For example, some people fast in groups, on scheduled days, and for varying lengths of time. Some fasts include giving up daily meals, sweets, coffee, television, all food, etc. I will share my fasting experiences and some that are found in Scripture.

In the book of Daniel, Daniel and the three other young men chose to fast from the food and drink they were served. They simply asked for a diet that met their convictions. God not only met their risky request, but He also blessed the results.

Jesus fasted for forty days in the wilderness from all food and drink.

The disciples had trouble casting out an unclean spirit, and Christ tells them that kind only comes forth by prayer and fasting.

There is a need for prayer and fasting for some victories to occur, whether spiritual or physical. You may be faithful to pray and take every need and request to the Lord, but are you fasting?

Fasting helps you focus on the Lord and fellowship with Him deeper. It is giving up something temporal to gain something eternal. Please do not consider this something you "have to endure." Fasting is a privilege! Why put off something that will lead to a closer walk with Jesus? Is temporarily giving up food, sugar, coffee, online shopping, social media, etc., a big deal compared to answered prayer and getting closer to Jesus?

In John 15, Christ invites you to Him. He explains you need to abide in Him and for Him to abide in you. This is His desire! He wants a close, intimate relationship with each of His children! The Creator of the universe, the Saviour that healed the sick, the One that died for you, desires to spend time with you! How incredible!

God has led me to fast a few times in my life. Each time was for someone else. Or so I thought. While He did work on the other person's behalf, He worked in my heart in ways I never imagined. Getting to experience such closeness with Him was worth everything He asked me to give up! Temporary discomforts are nothing in comparison to getting closer to Christ!

Sometimes you start fasting from one thing, like sugar, and before it's over, God asks for your coffee and social media, too. That's okay! Let Him have it! If you feel God is calling you to fast, do it joyfully and expectantly. Fasting is a blessing. Do not focus on what He's asking you to give up. Instead, focus on what you will learn!

My personal experience: When the 40-Day Sugar Fast became coffee and social media, too. My friend and fellow author, Wendy Speake, leads a community-wide sugar fast. She wrote *The 40-Day Sugar Fast* and *The 40-Day Social Media Fast.* I had started the sugar fast for the second time and knew I wanted to do the social media fast afterward. Halfway through the sugar fast, I felt God tugging at my heart. I needed to start the social media fast right then.

Fasting from social media was hard because I have a direct sales business that relies on social media. Not being present for 40 whole days could significantly hurt my business and the income I make with it. But God said to trust Him. I also have an Instagram page with a large community on it. What would happen if I didn't post for 40 days? Would I lose followers? God said to trust Him. So, I deleted the apps from my phone without posting why I would be absent. Then, God said He wanted my coffee too. *"Really, God? Are You sure?"* I thought. He was. I didn't need coffee to do my devotions. I didn't need coffee to get through the day. I didn't need coffee to homeschool. I needed Jesus.

The time without social media was SO freeing. I had so much free time, and less mental and emotional exhaustion. It was great. I missed it, but it was excellent at the same time. The result? I walked with Jesus for 80 days without distraction. My Instagram actually grew in those 40 days. My direct sales business is still going strong three years later. He took care of the details.

The first time I faced a trial and felt God leading me to fast was before the sugar fast incident. I just knew God was calling me to fast. He kept taking me to Matthew 17, where I have a note from a sermon that says, "If someone else's spiritual battle depends on my prayer and fasting, will they get the victory?" I knew I had to fast and pray. I had no clue how to fast, if there was a wrong way, how long it would last, or what I was giving up. So, I prayed. God took all food for four and a half days. I had one cup of coffee in the morning and water after that. I don't even like water, but God said to trust Him. I did, and it was the best four and a half days ever—such close intimacy with Him! I couldn't wait to have time to pray throughout the day. I wish I could say that God gave complete victory right then, but He didn't. Instead, I learned to trust Him and to pray with my hands open because I can't hold onto things. I must give them to the Lord. I was reminded that God loves me unconditionally, even in my sin. Romans 5:8 and 1 Peter 4:8 became so real to me. That is the abundant Christian life—more of Jesus.

While I would not have chosen to give up food, I would never want to say no to strengthening my faith and personal walk with Christ. If He's calling you to fast, just trust Him. It will be worth it.

Dear Lord,
Thank You for Your Word and Holy Spirit. Thank You for seeing every aspect of every battle we face. Help me to count it a privilege to fast and pray, whether for myself or others. I don't want to ever hold on to something tighter than I do in my relationship with You. Thank You for the privilege of prayer and fasting.
In Christ's name,
Amen.

Day Fifteen

Living Abundantly Through Charity

First Corinthians chapter 13 perfectly defines this word. This passage is one of the places you can replace *charity* with your name. If it fits, that's great! But most of us can't completely align with this chapter and have some work to do. Myself included. As Christians, charity should be a prominent characteristic of our lives. We want to be shown charity, but we aren't always quick to show it to others.

Webster's 1828 Dictionary defines charity this way: In a general sense, love, benevolence, good will; that disposition of heart which inclines men to think favorably of their fellow man, and to do them good. In a theological sense, it includes supreme love to God, and universal goodwill to men.

Living in charity toward others reminds you of how Christ loves you. This love is how you experience abundant Christian life and show Jesus to others in practical ways. Remember that the world views Jesus as unreal or untouchable. They believe He may exist; if He does, He's only accessible to certain people. It is up to those who truly know Him to show them how close and personal our Lord is! The lost need Him, and regardless of where they are, Jesus loves them. He wants to save them and have a relationship with them. They need to know that. The best way for them to know that is to see it lived and experienced practically and faithfully by you. Charity is an essential part of your testimony.

First Corinthians 8:1 says, "Now as touching things offered unto idols, we know that we all have knowledge. Knowledge puffeth up, but charity edifieth." Paul points out that knowledge can cause you to think you are above others, but love builds. As you will see, charity and pride do not coexist.

First Corinthians 16:14 says, "Let all your things be done in charity."

Charity is a command, not a suggestion. In First Corinthians 16:14, all means all. Your marriage, parenting, job, and ministry should all be done in charity. This is a challenging task. How do you show charity or love to those that make it complicated? How do you show charity in a job you dread going to? Or in a ministry that you do not feel qualified for? How do you do this when you have hard days and just do not feel like being very loving? Simply, through Christ. Philippians 4:13 says, "I can do all things through Christ which strengtheneth me." Again, all means all. You must be walking with Him each day. Praying, studying His Word, and being encouraged through godly preaching, music, and friends are all essential to keep us looking to Christ and following His Word. God teaches that there are blessings in obedience.

Charity requires action. You cannot simply say you love or care for someone if you never do anything to show that. Christ displayed His love for you by publicly dying on Calvary for your sins (John 3:16). You have probably heard the saying, "People don't care how much you know until they know how much you care." It is so very true. If someone does not feel cared for or loved, they want nothing to do with anything you have to say to them, regardless of your message's validity or necessity.

Chapter 13 is between God speaking of the Church and its spiritual gifts in chapter 12 and chapter 14, discussing prophecy. God makes no mistakes. He shows the importance of the Church, using spiritual gifts for God within the Church, and giving God's truth to others. Charity binds them together and is essential to both topics, which Paul explains in chapter 13. Also, notice that many of these words end with the suffix "-eth," a present-tense verb. Charity is not a one-time thing; this is to be how you live each day. It's just who God wants you to be. This happens as you yield to the leading of the Holy Spirit in your life.

Verse 1, "Though I speak with the tongues of men and of angels, and have not charity, I am become as sounding brass, or a tinkling cymbal." It does not matter how well you speak, sing, or teach; it is annoying, useless noise without charity. No one wants to listen to that.

Verse 2, "And though I have the gift of prophecy, and understand all mysteries, and all knowledge; and though I have all faith, so that I could remove mountains, and have not charity, I am nothing." Without charity, you will not be effective, regardless of how much knowledge and understanding you have.

Verse 3, "And though I bestow all my goods to feed the poor, and though I give my body to be burned, and have not charity, it profiteth me nothing." You can give without charity, but it is useless. However, the opposite is also true. You cannot have charity and be selfish. Selfless, sacrificial love honors the Lord.

Verse 4, "Charity suffereth long, and is kind; charity envieth not; charity vaunteth not itself, is not puffed up," Charity supports, endures, or sustains for long periods. It does not quit easily. Charity does not give up when things get hard or uncomfortable. It is steady and dependable. Charity stays, supports, encourages, and endures long-term. You may be facing a trial in your marriage, health, finances, or with your children. I do not know how long "long-term" is for you, but the Lord does. Remember to wait on Him, not on the outcome you want. This will not always be easy, but it can lead you closer to Christ if you let it. Longsuffering is also part of the fruit of the Spirit that God wants to cultivate in your life. This is not something you can genuinely produce on your own. Our flesh does not want to be longsuffering. Let Ephesians 4:2, Psalm 86:15, 2 Peter 2:15, and

Exodus 34:6 remind you of God's longsuffering toward you, even though you do not deserve it.

Charity is also kind. This is to do good to others, to make them happy by granting their requests, supplying wants, assisting in distress, having tenderness or goodness, and being benevolent. This is more than just not being rude or antisocial. Do you seek to help others in their distress? Or do you try to keep your distance and not get involved? For me, the second option is my natural tendency. It takes effort and energy to get involved. It takes vulnerability because your help or advice may get rejected. There's also a genuine fear of being taken advantage of.

However, that is not being Christ-like. Imagine if Christ didn't want to get too involved in your salvation or earthly distresses. You would be in a huge mess! Follow His leading as He shows you how to help others and what your kindness should look like in each situation, and then trust Him with the results. See also Romans 12:15, Ephesians 4:32, and Colossians 3:12.

Charity envieth not. Envy is very destructive, and it takes us only a short time to figure that out. Envy is to feel uneasiness, mortification, or discontent at the sight of superior excellence, reputation, or happiness enjoyed by another; to repine at another's prosperity; to fret or grieve one's self at the real or supposed superiority of another, and to hate him on that account.

Ouch. Hate is a strong word, isn't it? When I read that definition, I picture a temper tantrum—being mad and hating someone because they received something you did not. This behavior is the opposite of what Scripture teaches.

Envy and hate are the complete opposite of charity. Envy is closely related to jealousy. Even worse, this is accusing God of being unfair. Envy feels as if others are blessed, but you are left out. It is telling God that He is short-changing you and wrongfully blessing others. That is quite an attitude to have towards the Lord. Do not question God's blessings to anyone! See Proverbs 14:30, 1 Peter 2:1, Proverbs 23:17, and Galatians 5:26.

Charity vaunteth not itself. To vaunt is to boast; to make a vain display of what one is, has, or has done. To vaunt is to be full of oneself, taking credit for all accomplishments and doings. No one is self-made. Everything you are, have, and have done is because of God's grace. See Ephesians 2:8-9, Proverbs 27:1, and John 15:5.

Charity is not puffed up. Puffed up is to be driven out suddenly, as air or breath; blown up; swelled with air; inflated with vanity or pride; praised. This is not to say that all praise is wrong, but praising yourself is wrong. Refrain from building yourself up to look better than others. When you are puffed up, there's no real substance or security. This is the opposite of humility. Charity builds up others, not self. See also Philippians 2:3-4, 1 Peter 5:6, and Ephesians 4:2.

Verse 5, "Doth not behave itself unseemly, seeketh not her own, is not easily provoked, thinketh no evil;" Charity doth not behave itself unseemly. Unseemly is not fit or becoming; uncomely; unbecoming; indecent. What is unseemly to you may not be to someone else. This is why you are to use Scripture rather than your opinion. Truth does not change. The word that really caught my attention in this was "indecent." Indecent is unfit to be seen or heard; offensive to modesty and delicacy. The way you treat others should not be offensive, rude, harsh, or embarrassing. Your actions and reactions should be fitting for Christian character. See also 2 Timothy 2:21.

Charity seeketh not her own. To seek is to go in search or quest of; to search for by going from place to place. The wording here is very vivid. It shows that when you seek your own selfish happiness and satisfaction, you will not find it. You will go from place to place, never finding joy or contentment. God does not bless selfishness. The abundant life is found when you seek to bless others instead of pursuing your own desires. Jesus is the example of this lifestyle. His joy came from doing the will of God, which was always ministering to others. The will of God is where joy is found. See Philippians 2:3-4, Galatians 6:2, Psalm 37:4, and Romans 12:10.

Charity is not easily provoked. Provoke means to call to action; to arouse; to excite; as to provoke to anger or wrath by offensive words or injury. Ephesians 6:4 and Colossians 3:21 are for parents not to provoke children to anger. The most basic definition would be "to cause." You can provoke others to wrath, discouragement, and fear. But there is a positive side to this word to focus on. Hebrews 10:24 says to provoke one another to love and good works. Charity does not cause others hurt or anger through its actions or words. Remember that you significantly impact those around you. Charity is not easily angered, excited, or affected by others. Charity is consistent and stable. Charity keeps control of itself. Maintaining your emotions, views, and attitude amid others' negativity is a challenge worth accepting.

You do not have to match the attitudes of those around you. You do not have to live by emotions. You do not have to change your views and opinions to match those of society. You can be the steady and calm one in any situation.

Charity thinketh no evil. To think is to have the mind occupied on some subject; to have ideas, or to revolve ideas in the mind. Thinking is a continual dwelling on something. Evil has many definitions and examples but is simply the opposite of moral or good. Charity does not think wickedly, hoping for harm or negative things to happen to another person.

Verse 6 says, "Rejoiceth not in iniquity, but rejoiceth in the truth;"

Iniquity is injustice; unrighteous; a sin or crime; an act of injustice. Charity seeks what is right and good. It does not rejoice in what is bad or wrong. To rejoice in someone being treated unjustly or committing sin and crimes is not love. Charity rejoices in and seeks truth.

This also leads others to the truth as well. If you encourage someone's sin, you do not love them. True love gives the truth. Your standard of right and wrong should come from Scripture. If God says something is wrong, it's wrong.

Verse 7 says, "Beareth all things, believeth all things, hopeth all things, endureth all things." Beareth is to carry, convey, or support. To bear is not suggesting supporting sin. Keep it in the context of being like Christ and rejoicing in the truth. You need the help and wisdom of God in all areas, including this one. See why prayer and Bible study are so important? Your flesh doesn't always want to bear through things. Quitting is an easier option in some cases. Loving sinful, hurt, angry, bitter, unlovely people is hard, but you are called to love like Christ. So often, genuinely loving people brings them to Christ, and He works out the details. That's the goal, isn't it? Not to clean them up yourself but to get them to the Lord. Never forget Christ's love for you and that it's the same love He had for you before salvation.

Charity believeth all things. Believeth is the present tense of giving credit to testimony or to evidence other than personal knowledge. Keep this in context. This is not blindly believing and accepting anything anyone says at any time, but it is also not believing false teachings contradictory to Scripture. It is giving the benefit of the doubt, not forming an opinion of someone based on what others say, and not spreading gossip. Slandering someone's reputation is not charity. Thinking negatively of another person because of gossip is not charity. Charity takes Scripture as the final authority, and God deals with gossip and lies—resulting in Christ being Lord of your life, thus fulfilling the other attributes and honoring Him. This is the key to an abundant life.

Charity hopeth all things. Hopeth is having a desire of some good, accompanied with at least a slight expectation of obtaining it, or a belief that it is obtainable. Hope differs from a wish in that hope implies an expectation of obtaining the desired thing. A wish is more of an attitude that the thing desired is just a dream, not expected in reality. It is confidence in a future event; the highest degree of well-founded expectation of good; as a hope founded on God's gracious promises; a scriptural sense. It is an expected assurance that God's promises are true. Trusting God leads to abundant life and wisdom in all other areas. Trusting God keeps you from trusting yourself and being led by the flesh.

Charity endureth all things. Endureth is to last; to continue in the same state without perishing; to remain; to abide. Is this not how God's love is? It is unconditional and unchanging.

Charity never faileth. Faileth means to become deficient; to be insufficient; to cease to be abundant for supply; or to be entirely wanting.

When you apply these to your life, and choose to love like Christ, love will not be insufficient. This love brings people to Jesus, honors Him, and makes Him visible to others through you. Be a vessel. You can't manufacture this type of love in and of yourself.

It has to be His love in and through you, or it will fall short. True love is sacrificial, but it is biblical and always worth it. Great things will happen when you live in biblical charity. God will bless and enable you to keep loving as He does. You will experience God working in and through you to bless and help others. Loving God and loving others is truly the abundant Christian life.

Heavenly Father,
I know Your love is unchanging, unconditional, and all-sufficient. This is not the type of love I naturally want to show others. This love is inconvenient at times and always sacrificial. I am thankful you never tire of loving me. Father, please help me to be a willing vessel. Help me to love like Christ and point others to You. Strengthen and guide me in biblical charity. Thank You again for Your perfect love.
In Christ's name,
Amen.

Day Sixteen

Living Abundantly Through Your Testimony

Romans 1:16, "For I am not ashamed of the gospel of Christ: for it is the power of God unto salvation to every one that believeth; to the Jew first, and also to the Greek."

Acts 22:15, "For thou shalt be his witnesses unto all men of what thou hast seen and heard."

Your testimony is valuable. It does not matter if God saved you as a five-year-old child or a fifty-five-year-old addict. All salvations are miracles and need to be shared. I was saved as a 13-year-old who was not raised in church. Your testimony may be similar. Others need to know that salvation happens outside the church walls and is just as authentic as salvation inside the church. God is not limited in His saving abilities. People are looking for something real, something substantial to put their faith and hope in. The world needs to see that God loves them. We all have different stories which God wants to use. You may think your testimony is dull, simple, or unexciting, but someone needs to hear it to know that they, too,

can be saved and have the abundant life Christ offers!
You do not have to find Christ in the prison cell,
hospital, or rehab facility to have a powerful testimony.
Share with others what God has done for you. It really
is that simple.

As a child, I visited a few churches here and
there with a friend or family member, but nothing
memorable stood out. Even in those moments, I can
see God was planting a seed. I knew something was
different about the church, even though I did not know
all the details. When I was 13, my mom wanted to
start attending church. She would take my sister and
me with her, but attendance was inconsistent. One
Saturday morning, a man from the church knocked on
the front door. He was out on visitation and wanted to
thank us for coming. He asked if we needed anything
or had any questions for him. Before he left, he asked
if we knew for sure that we would go to Heaven if we
died. My mom, sister, and I all said no. He opened the
Bible, read a few verses, asked us questions, and
explained what he had read. One at a time, we
prayed and asked the Lord to save us that morning in
the living room. I can't speak for my mom and sister,
but I am saved. A few weeks later, we were baptized
together at church.

Uneventful, yet miraculous. Jesus did not have
to save me just because I asked Him to. But He did
because that is what Scripture promises. Jesus wants
everyone to be saved. Sometimes the simple and
uneventful testimonies are what will bring others to

Jesus. Do not be afraid to speak for God and to praise Him through sharing your testimony.

Dear God,
It can be challenging to share my testimony. Sometimes I get nervous or don't know how to share it. But I know that You saved me, and I know You want to save those around me as well. Please give me wisdom, clarity, and opportunities to share my salvation testimony. Help me to bring others to You so they may also receive salvation and the abundant Christian life. Thank You for saving and loving me.
In Christ's name,
Amen.

Day Seventeen

Living Abundantly Through Godly Speech

The Bible has much to say about your words. Once the words leave your mouth or you hit send on a text, they can't be taken back. Your speech can encourage others or tear them down. You can praise God and His doings or deny Him and take the praise for yourself.

Proverbs 15:1 says, "A soft answer turneth away wrath: but grievous words stir up anger." This verse is usually applied to the person receiving the words. Words can turn away wrath or stir anger in the hearer. But the same is true for the speaker. If your words or tone get angry, it escalates the situation, and you get more worked up. The opposite is also true. You do not get as worked up if your words are kind and your tone soft.

Proverbs 31:26 says, "She openeth her mouth with wisdom; and in her tongue is the law of kindness." This should be your desire for your speech. Let wisdom and kindness be what flows from your lips.

David said in Psalm 141:3, "Set a watch, O LORD, before my mouth; keep the door of my lips." You should pray for your words and tone often. God wants to help in this area. James 1:19-20 says, "Wherefore, my beloved brethren, let every man be swift to hear, slow to speak, slow to wrath: For the wrath of man worketh not the righteousness of God."

Later, in chapter 3, verses 5-10 say, "Even so the tongue is a little member, and boasteth great things. Behold, how great a matter a little fire kindleth! And the tongue is a fire, a world of iniquity: so is the tongue among our members, that it defileth the whole body, and setteth on fire the course of nature; and it is set on fire of hell. For every kind of beasts, and of birds, and of serpents, and of things in the sea, is tamed, and hath been tamed of mankind: But the tongue can no man tame; it is an unruly evil, full of deadly poison. Therewith bless we God, even the Father; and therewith curse we men, which are made after the similitude of God. Out of the same mouth proceedeth blessing and cursing. My brethren, these things ought not so to be." God is clear that His help is needed in this matter and that words are powerful.

Over and over in Psalms, God says to praise Him, offer thanksgiving, and cry out to Him. Scripture is one constant story of God, all He has done, and how He has shown His love. When you see His goodness and faithfulness, this should lead you to praise Him. God wants you to use your words to communicate with Him. Praise, thanksgiving, and anything you say that honors God is worship. This does not come naturally. This takes being intentional and obeying the leading of the Holy Spirit.

Additionally, He wants you to use your words to communicate what He has done for you to others. There will be times when you just don't feel like you can keep going. It may be any number of trials, valleys, or intense spiritual warfare. When you are tired and weak, you may not have much faith to stand on, but when a brother or sister in Christ shares praise or testimony, it encourages you to keep going and trusting. Sometimes you must stand on their faith for a bit, which is okay. Sharing what God has done for you allows a struggling Christian to be strengthened and encouraged by your faith.

Share what God has done for you, including the trials. I don't want to admit that my husband and I argued, that my kids are being difficult, or that I am dealing with spiritual warfare. But you know what? Keeping that trial and victory private doesn't help anyone. I am not saying to share every detail of your life. But I am saying that a hurting brother or sister needs to know they're not alone and that their valley can have comfort and victory. They need to know you have walked through that same valley and survived by the grace of God.

It's also a good reminder of what God has done. Telling others strengthens your faith as well as theirs. Seek to live abundantly by telling others what God has done for you.

Dear Heavenly Father,
Thank You for Your many blessings in my life. So
many times, You have protected, provided, and given
me grace, mercy, and wisdom. Thank You for inviting
me to come into Your presence to pray and worship.
You have been too good to me for me to keep quiet
about what You have done. Father, I pray You would
give me the opportunity and courage to tell others
what You have done. Forgive me for keeping Your
goodness to myself. May I use my words for praise,
prayer, worship, and encouragement.
In Jesus' Name,
Amen.

Day Eighteen

Living Abundantly Through Witnessing

Acts 1:8, "But ye shall receive power, after that the Holy Ghost is come upon you: and ye shall be witnesses unto me both in Jerusalem, and in all Judaea, and in Samaria, and unto the uttermost part of the earth."

"For whosoever shall call upon the name of the Lord shall be saved. How then shall they call on him in whom they have not believed? and how shall they believe in him of whom they have not heard? and how shall they hear without a preacher? And how shall they preach, except they be sent? as it is written, How beautiful are the feet of them that preach the gospel of peace, and bring glad tidings of good things!" Romans 10:13-15

"The fruit of the righteous is a tree of life; and he that winneth souls is wise." Proverbs 11:30

What could be better than bringing others to Jesus? To know someone will be in Heaven forever because you took the time to share the Gospel with them is the highest form of love you can offer. Sadly schedules and fear of rejection get in the way of witnessing.

Are you saved and on your way to Heaven right now? If you are, it's because of God and someone obeying His leading to tell you about your need for a Saviour. God commands all Christians to be soul winners. This is not just for the pastor, deacon, or evangelist. You do not have to be highly educated, a great speaker, or a Bible scholar. You just have to form relationships with people, see them as an eternal soul with an eternal destination, pray for God's help, and obey His leading. You know how you got saved; that is enough to tell someone else how to be saved.

Keeping your relationship with God to yourself helps no one. There is joy in witnessing. Every soul that gets saved is a miracle, and you get to be a part of it! God doesn't have to use you, but He chooses to! Don't ever forget that or take it for granted.

Another reason for not telling others about eternity and salvation is due to complacency. Have you gotten over your salvation? Have you forgotten when Jesus heard your cry and saved your soul from Hell? Take time over the next few days to return to that place. Maybe you can visit the physical location of your salvation. If not, go there mentally. Remember where you were, how you felt, the days leading up to your salvation, and who was there. Do you remember the weight of your sin being lifted? Do you remember the joy you had knowing Jesus loved you and forgave you? Do you *really* remember? Then tell someone and help them experience Jesus the same way you did! Live abundantly through witnessing by witnessing abundantly. He desires for all to be saved.

Witnessing must be a matter of prayer and intentionality. Pray for God's help. Ask Him to give you the courage to talk to others or hand them a tract. Be prepared. Carry tracts in your purse, car, or suit coat. If you don't have them, you can't give them out. Leave it on the table for your server when you go out to eat. Leave one on the bathroom sink after you wash your hands. Give one to the lady at the check-out or drive-thru window. The opportunities are endless. You just have to take the time to see them. There's no conversation you could have that is more important than that of eternity.

Dear Lord,
Thank You for saving my soul. Thank You that someone shared the Good News with me, and I cried out to You for salvation. Thank You for Calvary, for paying my sin debt before I ever asked. Thank You for Your love. Father, help me to share this wonderful gift with others. Help me to see people as souls that need saving. Give me the courage to share the Gospel.
In Jesus' name,
Amen.

Day Nineteen

Living Abundantly Through Sacrifice

The word "sacrifice" brings a few things to mind. First would be the Old Testament sacrifices and offerings. Next would be the idea of giving something up. Sacrifice is "an act of slaughtering an animal or person or surrendering a possession as an offering to God or to a divine or supernatural figure."

This is a voluntary act. You are choosing to surrender or kill something. Today, God does not require us to offer those animal sacrifices. But we still have to kill and surrender things. We must kill our flesh's ungodly desires and sinful habits. This is not always easy, nor is it always a one-time situation. You should also surrender to His will rather than your own. Surrendering what you can see for what you can't is faith.

Scripture has a lot to say about sacrifices and surrender.

"I beseech you therefore, brethren, by the mercies of God, that ye present your bodies a living sacrifice, holy, acceptable unto God, which is your reasonable service." Romans 12:1

"Offer the sacrifices of righteousness, and put your trust in the Lord." Psalm 4:5.

"By him therefore let us offer the sacrifice of praise to God continually, that is, the fruit of our lips giving thanks to his name." Hebrews 13:15.

Your life should be a sacrifice to the Lord. Living in surrender is giving up your way, will, and plans for His. This is how to live the abundant Christian life. Trusting God and following Him will lead you to do and live through things you cannot imagine. It may be challenging, even painful, to surrender something to the Lord, but it is always worth it.

Talk to any pastor, evangelist, missionary, married couple, or anyone else living for and serving God. Ask what they have endured and how they made it. They'll tell you it's the grace of God. People don't leave their country and home to live among strangers on a whim. People don't stay married for years by accident and luck. Pastors don't stay behind their pulpits for money and recognition. It's sacrifice and surrender.

As a homeschool mom, I can say that we do this out of surrender and faith. I could enroll my kids in the Christian school at our church and get a job. But that is not God's will for our family. We have said yes to His leading and given up being a two-income household. Would we like to have the extra money? Of course. Are we barely scraping by? No. Because God is faithful and has taken care of us. Does it make sense or add up on paper? Only sometimes. It doesn't have to. God owns the cattle on a thousand hills and the wealth in every mine. I don't have to worry about giving anything up to be in His will, nor do you.

Sacrifice and surrender are not bad words, nor does it lead to poverty. It leads to growth, stronger faith, and a deeper walk with Jesus. Not more stuff, more prestige, or more money. Just more of Jesus. Giving up anything that draws you away from Christ will always lead to an abundant life.

Dear Lord,
Thank You for Your leading in my life. Thank You for showing me things that I need to put down. There's nothing I desire more than a closer walk with You. Some habits are hard to break, and giving up my will for Yours is not always easy. But I know You love me and want me to live in faith and obedience. Help me to live a life of surrender to You.
In Jesus' name,
Amen.

Day Twenty

Living Abundantly Through Service

"For, brethren, ye have been called unto liberty; only use not liberty for an occasion to the flesh, but by love serve one another." Galatians 5:13

Christ is the example of living a life of service. "Even as the Son of man came not to be ministered unto, but to minister, and to give his life a ransom for many." Matthew 20:28

Service is not a position most people are seeking to take on. Your flesh and society tell you to be a leader, to seek the highest positions, and to do anything but serve, and if you do serve, to be self-serving. Serving others is the last thing your flesh usually wants to do. You will not see the media telling you to put yourself last.

Thankfully, you don't have to live by the world's standards. With Jesus being the highest example, throughout the Bible, God teaches that serving others should be a characteristic of every Christian.

Whatever you are doing, do it well and thoroughly. Half-done service is not service that honors the Lord.

There's nothing too low for you to do for the Lord. Anything you do for your family, church, or a stranger can be service to God. It is easy to get caught up in the day-to-day things and just go through the motions. Every meal made, every article of clothing washed, and every minute of homeschooling and homework is also service to Jesus and should be done diligently.

Adopting this attitude every day will change your life. Your temper would be lost less often, the laundry folded sooner, joy found in everyday tasks, and you would show more kindness to strangers. If cleaning toilets, calling a widow, making a meal, or being there for a hurting friend is "below" you, then you need to spend time with the Lord and reevaluate your priorities.

Jesus does not have to use you to accomplish His will or show His love to someone that may not know Him, but He does. Be a vessel God can use. Be willing to say yes when He asks you to do something. There is joy in serving Jesus. That service starts right where you are, in your home and church. God will not call you to "bigger" things such as missionary work, teaching, or leading some ministry if you don't obey what He has already given you.

Choose to be an encouragement, a prayer warrior, and faithful to where God has you. Nothing is too small to be done for the glory of God. Others are watching you and learning from your example. May they learn to joyfully serve, too.

Dear Heavenly Father,
Thank You for using me to accomplish Your perfect
will. Please help me to see the tasks I have to do as
things I get to do for You. From caring for my home
and family to encouraging others, it should all be done
unto You. May my life show others that Jesus loves
them and there is joy in serving.
In the name of Jesus,
Amen.

Day Twenty-One

Living Abundantly Through Humility

God hates pride. Pride is part of your sinful nature. God knows this and has given many verses to help you understand yourself better.

Pride is "a feeling of deep pleasure or satisfaction derived from one's own achievements, the achievements of those with whom one is closely associated, or from qualities or possessions that are widely admired."

Pride is the opposite of depending on God and giving Him praise, glory, and recognition for everything.

"Pride goeth before destruction, and an haughty spirit before a fall." Proverbs 16:18

"When pride cometh, then cometh shame: but with the lowly is wisdom." Proverbs 11:2

"Only by pride cometh contention: but with the well advised is wisdom." Proverbs 13:10

"But he giveth more grace. Wherefore he saith, God resisteth the proud, but giveth grace unto the humble." James 4:6

Humility is "a modest or low view of one's own importance; humbleness."

There's a quote by C.S. Lewis that explains this well. "Humility is not thinking less of yourself, it's thinking of yourself less."

"Humble yourselves therefore under the mighty hand of God, that he may exalt you in due time:" 1 Peter 5:6

"Likewise, ye younger, submit yourselves unto the elder. Yea, all of you be subject one to another, and be clothed with humility: for God resisteth the proud, and giveth grace to the humble." 1 Peter 5:5

"By humility and the fear of the Lord are riches, and honour, and life." Proverbs 22:4

A life of lifting yourself up and seeking the praise of others is a life of no lasting reward. Living in such a way that honors God, glorifies Him, brings others to Him, and says, "He is worthy to be praised and trusted" should be the life you seek to live.

John 3:30 says, "He must increase, but I must decrease." This really should be the goal of every Christian. It is not about what you do, but what God does in and through you. You are just a vessel. It is always about the Saviour. I hope you will choose to trust Him and live for His honor and glory rather than your own. Humility is truly the path to living an abundant life in Christ.

Dear Jesus,
Thank You for your everlasting love, forgiveness, grace, and very present help. I struggle with my flesh and sinful pride. Father, I desire to live a life that honors You. May I live in the shadow of the cross, pointing others to the spotless Lamb of God rather than to myself. Thank You for being worthy of all praise and trust. You are faithful.
In Jesus' Name,
Amen.

Day Twenty-Two

Living Abundantly Through Health Challenges

"For ye are bought with a price: therefore glorify God in your body, and in your spirit, which are God's." 1 Corinthians 6:20

"And we know that all things work together for good to them that love God, to them who are the called according to his purpose." Romans 8:28

"And said, Naked came I out of my mother's womb, and naked shall I return thither: the Lord gave, and the Lord hath taken away; blessed be the name of the Lord." Job 1:21

No one hopes, prays, or asks for poor health, nor does anyone want to watch a loved one endure a health trial. However, perfect health is not always God's plan for your life. It helps to remember that everything belongs to Him, including your health. God is honored when you learn to trust, praise, worship, and witness through these trials. Praising God is easy when things are going well, but you must also learn to praise Him when the trials come. Praising, trusting, worshiping, and witnessing can be hard when you have experienced that dreaded phone call that says things like "cancer," "fibromyalgia," "we aren't sure," or "there's nothing we can do." It is not easy to hear or accept these things.

Chances are, you have a health challenge, whether yours or a loved one's. Others may or may not even know.

In December of 2008, I delivered our first baby fourteen weeks early. Seeing him with all the tubes and wires, knowing I could do nothing to help him felt impossible. Then, In March of 2016, I delivered our daughter five weeks early. Again with the NICU stay and helplessness.

In 2017 my husband was diagnosed with Hashimoto's disease. In 2020, at 27 years old, I was diagnosed with fibromyalgia. In 2022, at 29 years old, I was told I had polycystic ovarian syndrome (PCOS), which explained many symptoms I experienced. Sometimes it is a relief to have an answer so you can move forward, but it is still hard to hear the finality of something being truly wrong. I understand that our health challenges are small compared to many others, but I still want to encourage you to glorify God this season, rest in Him, and let Him be the source of your joy, even in pain or sickness and the unknown.

I am so thankful that I can praise God for knowing these trials would come. Knowing that nothing takes my Saviour by surprise is a comfort to me. Having confidence that He loves my husband and children more than I do helps me trust Him when they struggle. Trusting that He already knows the outcome and how this will work for your good, should drive you to praise, worship, and witness.

You are not the only one struggling. Someone else needs your faith and encouragement through their trial, too. Learn to praise God in any circumstance publicly. Sometimes, your faith is small, and you must rest in someone else's and vice versa. That is what the body of Christ is for! To pray for and edify one another!

God is still God. Not one ounce of His goodness, love, wisdom, or sovereignty is lost because you are in a trial.

You rely on your health for everything. It is how you function. God wants you to care for your physical, mental, emotional, and spiritual health. When any of these are neglected, you notice it. Things are just off. You struggle to do the things you need to do when you don't get enough sleep or get sick. Simple things seem impossible. When your spiritual health is neglected, God is not in His proper place of preeminence. Then church, prayer, and Bible reading are neglected, causing you to be unprepared for Satan's attacks because you are vulnerable. You must maintain these areas the best you can.

But, sometimes, God allows sickness to come. This is where you get to live out your faith. During illness, you get to *really* live a life that says God is still good, that He is enough, and that He can be trusted. He has promised never to leave nor forsake you. Believing this promise leads you to live abundantly during health challenges. There are Bible passages and songs that will never feel real to you until you need them, but when the time comes, they'll be there.

Learn to worship and sing "It Is Well With My Soul" during a health challenge. It's not easy. But if you can truly trust God and honestly believe that it is well, you will be able to praise God and draw others to Him in ways you never could before! You may never be able to grasp that God is an ever-present help in time of need until you are the one in need! (Hebrews 4:16) Let your health challenges bring you to God rather than using them as a reason to turn away from Him. Take time to read the stories of the hymns and the saints of the past. Many have testimonies of physical ailments with no cure or relief, yet they experienced and responded to God in ways you could never imagine.

Learn to trust, praise, worship, and witness in life's circumstances. Let challenges draw you closer to the Lord. Choose to trust Him and live abundantly, even in health challenges.

Dear Abba Father,
I am thankful that You are always with me. There's
nothing that I ever have to endure alone. Thank You
for only allowing things in my life for my good and
Your glory. Please help me trust, praise, worship, and
witness through any health challenge I face. Forgive
me when I fail. Draw me close to You, so You may
strengthen me and draw others to You.
In the precious name of Christ,
Amen.

Day Twenty-Three

Living Abundantly Through Trials

Trials are things you would never ask for. But, as you probably know, the Christian life is often characterized and strengthened by trials. You've heard the old saying that you're either in a trial, just out of one, or one is coming. How true that is! But you can and should be thankful for those trials.

Every trial comes through God's hand. Trials do not change Him, meaning He is still in control and on the throne. "Jesus Christ the same yesterday, and to day, and for ever." Hebrews 13:8 Trials can either draw us closer to God or further away from Him, but that choice is yours.

Even in trials, He doesn't move away from you. Psalm 46:1 "God is our refuge and strength, a very present help in trouble." Trials allow you to go deeper in your prayer life and in your understanding of Who He is. They also allow you to be a testimony of His goodness and power. Sometimes your trials are more for others than you. Maybe someone else needs to see God work, and He chooses to do that through you. It could be that the trial is for you, but later, you'll meet someone else in a similar situation, and you can encourage them through it.

Don't despise the trials. Romans 8:28 says, "And we know that all things work together for good to them that love God, to them who are the called according to his purpose." James 1:2-3 says, "My brethren, count it all joy when ye fall into divers temptations; Knowing this, that the trying of your faith worketh patience."

Nothing comes to you outside of God's knowledge or without a purpose. Trust Him even in the trials.

Dear Heavenly Father,
Thank You, Lord, for always being present. I know trials will come, and I pray that You will strengthen me through them. Help me to be a testimony of Your grace and goodness. You are so faithful to me. Please help me to remain faithful when my faith is tested and tried.
In Jesus' name,
Amen.

Day Twenty-Four

Living Abundantly Through Rest

"Come unto me, all ye that labour and are heavy laden, and I will give you rest. "Take my yoke upon you, and learn of me; for I am meek and lowly in heart: and ye shall find rest unto your souls." Matthew 11:28-29

"And he said, My presence shall go with thee, and I will give thee rest." Exodus 33:14

"There remaineth therefore a rest to the people of God." Hebrews 4:9

"And he said unto them, Come ye yourselves apart into a desert place, and rest a while: for there were many coming and going, and they had no leisure so much as to eat." Mark 6:31

It is tempting to compare your productivity with your spirituality or success. You are not what you accomplish! God does not base His love for you on your accomplishments! I am all for being busy for Jesus. We should be busy about the Father's business and the tasks He has called us to. However, rest is also biblical.

Jesus wants you to spend time with Him, and often that gets neglected when life gets busy. This should be your first form of rest, spending quiet time with the Saviour without distractions. He also gave an example of rest when He pulled away from the multitude. In Genesis, God rested on the seventh day. God was not tired; He was setting an example. Rest is biblical. Rest is not laziness or unfaithfulness; it is necessary. God does not want burnt-out Christians offering half-hearted service. Burnout leads to bitterness and resentment and, ultimately, quitting altogether. Do not let yourself get to that point of quitting on God because you didn't take time to rest.

God may be asking you to step down from a ministry. It may be temporary or permanent. Trust Him with this decision. He knows your heart, and He also knows what you need. Be careful not to put pressure on yourself that God never intended. If you are more concerned with what others will think of you for stepping down, you must shift your focus to Christ and what He asks you to do.

He may also lead you to fast from social media, sugar, caffeine, or communication with certain people. You may feel overwhelmed because of all the "extras." It's okay to set them down for a while and focus on your spiritual and physical health. Don't wait for a health crisis to force you to rest. Don't wait until an emergency to get your prayer life and devotions back on track.

Dear Lord,
Thank You for the example and reminder to rest. Life gets so busy, and there's always so much to do. Thank You for this reminder that rest is just as biblical as service. Help me to rest when needed. Please refresh and revive my spirit so I can continue faithfully serving You as You lead me. Thank You for loving me and caring about the details of my life.
In Jesus' name,
Amen.

Day Twenty-Five

Living Abundantly Through Meekness

Webster's 1828 dictionary defines meekness as "Softness of temper; mildness; gentleness; forbearance under injuries and provocations. Humility; resignations; submission to the divine will, without murmuring or peevishness."

Galatians 5:22 teaches this is part of the fruit of the Spirit. That means this is a characteristic God wants you to have in your life through the working of the Holy Spirit. You must yield to His work in you to exemplify this in your life.

Through the years, I have heard two simple thoughts about meekness. The first is my favorite: meekness is not weakness. The second says meekness is easily imposed upon.

Meekness is the opposite of pride and arrogance. Scripture gives many examples of meekness. First is the perfect example of Jesus Himself. Matthew 11:29 says, "Take my yoke upon you, and learn of me; for I am meek and lowly in heart: and ye shall find rest for your souls." Moses was also counted as being meek in Numbers 12:3, "(Now the man Moses was very meek, above all the men which were upon the face of the earth.)"

The Lord commands Christians to be meek and show a spirit of meekness to others. Ephesians 4:2, "With all lowliness and meekness, with longsuffering, forbearing one another in love;" Colossians 3:12, "Put on therefore, as the elect of God, holy and beloved, bowels of mercies, kindness, humbleness of mind, meekness, longsuffering;" "Wherefore lay apart all filthiness and superfluity of naughtiness, and receive with meekness the engrafted word, which is able to save your souls." James 1:21 "But thou, O man of God, flee these things; and follow after righteousness, godliness, faith, love, patience, meekness." 1 Timothy 6:11

You will not be teachable, grow spiritually, or show Christ to others if you are unwilling to be meek. Let God work in your life to produce this attribute for His honor and glory. You get to live abundantly when you live in obedience to God.

Abba Father,
Thank You, Father, for taking such time to teach me Your Word. Thank You for loving me enough to work in my life so I may be more like You. Please help me to remember that meekness is not weakness. Thank You for displaying this during Your earthly ministry. Father, help me to live a life of meekness.
In Jesus' name,
Amen.

Day Twenty-Six

Living Abundantly Through Gentleness

Ephesians 5:22 continues teaching on the fruit of the Spirit. Next is gentleness. Webster's 1828 defines this as "Softness of manners; mildness of temper; sweetness of disposition; meekness." Also, being gentle is not rough, harsh, or severe.

Does this describe you and your behavior? Are you a gentle person?

As we get closer to the coming of Christ in the clouds, the less gentle people are, including Christians.

Society has become rough, rude, hurried, and inconsiderate. Imagine if Christ had behaved that way during His life on earth. Roughness is not loving, welcoming, or inviting. People would not have been drawn to Him, lives would not have been changed, and Christianity as we know it would not exist.

Christ draws people to Him through His gentleness. He is not rough, harsh, or inconsiderate. When you are not gentle, you are not representing

Him well, nor do you cause others to draw close to Him.

It's usually easier to be gentle with strangers. Most people are good at being kind to those they don't know. However, you may lose that gentleness with those closest to you. Are you rough with your spouse, children, or dearest friends and expecting them to accept it? That behavior does not say, "I love you."

Gentleness is not passiveness. Gentleness does not throw out boundaries, firmness, and responsibility. Being gentle does not mean you are a pushover that no one will take seriously. Being gentle does not mean you have to whisper every instruction you give. It means that you are kind and considerate to those you interact with. Gentleness is not tearing others down to get your way.

It is not being gentle if you speak to others with threats, ultimatums, personal attacks, and insults. There is not a single word we say or think the Lord doesn't hear. He knows how you feel about and talk to others. Do your words please Him? Are your tone and comments reflecting the gentleness of Jesus?

Being gentle models Christ but it also brings blessings to your own life. The Lord will not allow you to be rough with others without consequence. Seek to be right with the Lord and others and experience abundant relationships by choosing gentleness.

Heavenly Father,
Thank You, Lord, for being the Gentle Shepherd that loves and leads His sheep. Your gentleness brings me comfort and security in my relationship with You. Help me to be gentle with those around me. Lord, please help me to live the abundant, Spirit-filled life that You have for me. May my words and actions be an accurate reflection of You. Thank You for being gentle with me. Please forgive me when I have failed to be gentle with others, show me any relationship where I need to ask for forgiveness from someone else, and help me to grow in this area.
In the gentle name of Jesus, I pray,
Amen.

Day Twenty-Seven

Living Abundantly Through Longsuffering

"With all lowliness and meekness, with longsuffering, forbearing one another in love;" Ephesians 4:2

"But the fruit of the Spirit is love, joy, peace, longsuffering, gentleness, goodness, faith," Galatians 5:22

"That ye might walk worthy of the Lord unto all pleasing, being fruitful in every good work, and increasing in the knowledge of God; Strengthened with all might, according to his glorious power, unto all patience and longsuffering with joyfulness;" Colossians 1:10-11

"But thou, O Lord, art a God full of compassion, and gracious, longsuffering, and plenteous in mercy and truth." Psalm 86:15

"And the Lord passed by before him, and proclaimed, The Lord, The Lord God, merciful and gracious, longsuffering, and abundant in goodness and truth, Keeping mercy for thousands, forgiving iniquity and transgression and sin, and that will by no means clear the guilty; visiting the iniquity of the fathers upon the children, and upon the children's children, unto the third and to the fourth generation." Exodus 34:6-7

This is a quality of the Lord and one that He wants to work in you. Unfortunately, this attribute does not come by accident. It is produced by trial. Longsuffering isn't fun, but it is essential to the Christian life.

Longsuffering is defined as "bearing injuries or provocation for a long time; patient; not easily provoked." This sounds like 1 Corinthians 13 and the Lord's description of charity. Just think of your life, your prayers for forgiveness, and the mistakes you continue to make. Yet, the Lord still loves you, does not respond in anger, and continues to forgive and help you. That is longsuffering.

God wants you to be this way with others. Maybe you have a spouse that does not share your religious beliefs, a wayward child, or a loved one that is difficult to get along with. These are all opportunities to grow in this area of longsuffering. You would not usually ask for this, but as with trials, it is needed. You cannot be longsuffering without God's help or praying for that person. Praying for someone changes your attitude toward them.

Choosing to be Christ-like and be longsuffering will help you to live an abundant Christian life. When you are longsuffering, you are walking in obedience to the Lord, bringing joy and blessings to your life.

Dear Jesus,
Being longsuffering can be challenging. My flesh wants to lash out at times or even give up on those that I need to be longsuffering with. Forgive me for falling short in this area. Thank You for being longsuffering and being my example and helper. Please help me to be as longsuffering with others as You are with me.
In Jesus' name,
Amen.

Day Twenty-Eight

Living Abundantly Through Peace

Everyone desires peace, yet very few people possess it or even know where to find it. Thankfully you have the True Source of peace: Jesus Christ. You do not have to hope and long for peace. Peace is not a mystical state that just happens to you. Peace is possible in all situations. Praise God for that!

I love the way Webster's 1828 dictionary defines peace: 1. In a general sense, a state of quiet or tranquility; freedom from disturbance or agitation; applicable to society, to individuals, or to the temper of the mind. 5. Freedom from agitation or disturbance by the passions, as from fear, terror, anger, anxiety or the like; quietness of mind; tranquility; calmness; quiet of conscience. 6. Heavenly rest; the happiness of heaven.

How wonderful does that sound? Now, let's look at the Bible and see what God says about this peace.

Psalm 199:165 says, "Great peace have they which love thy law: and nothing shall offend them." Do you love God's Word? Do you spend time in Scripture each day? You will lack peace if you neglect the Word of God.

Philippians 4:6-7 says, "Be careful for nothing; but in every thing by prayer and supplication with thanksgiving, let your requests be made known unto God. And the peace of God which passeth all understanding, shall keep your hearts and minds through Christ Jesus." Are you spending time in praise and prayer? Are you taking the time to talk to God and listen for Him to respond? God says to take everything to Him first. Everything. No exceptions. If you take every thought and care to others first, no wonder you lack peace! Once you truly grasp that God alone is the source of peace, you will run to Him first and more often.

Isaiah 26:3 is a wonderful promise from God. "Thou wilt keep him in perfect peace, whose mind is stayed on thee: because he trusteth in thee." Satan attacks our minds because it's easy. When you do not guard your mind, it is open to attack, and you experience fear, worry, panic, and instability. God wants your mind to be on Him. When you focus on Him, you learn to trust Him, and then you can experience His peace.

"Now the Lord of peace himself give you peace always by all means. The Lord be with you all." 2 Thessalonians 3:16

"These things I have spoken unto you, that in me ye might have peace. In the world ye shall have tribulation: but be of good cheer; I have overcome the world." John 16:33

"And let the peace of God rule in your hearts, to the which also ye are called in one body; and be ye thankful." Colossians 3:15

"For unto us a child is born, unto us a son is given: and the government shall be upon his shoulder: and his name shall be called Wonderful, Counsellor, The mighty God, The everlasting Father, The Prince of Peace." Isaiah 9:6

"And the work of righteousness shall be peace; and the effect of righteousness quietness and assurance for ever." Isaiah 32:17.

Isaiah 57:21 says, "There is no peace, saith my God, to the wicked." You cannot live in unrighteousness and live in peace at the same time.

When you live apart from God, there will not be any peace, and you will not experience the abundant life He came to bring. It takes time, intentionality, and work to be in God's Word, but it is worth it! Seek the peace of God today.

Dear Lord,
Thank You for being the Prince of Peace and coming to Earth for me. Thank You for giving peace that cannot be taken away. You are so loving, kind, and faithful. Thank You for caring about every detail of my life, down to my peace and joy. Father, I pray that You will forgive me for living apart from You and Your Word so often. Please help me to be faithful to spend time with You, to let Your Word dwell in me richly, and to experience Your peace.
In Jesus' name,
Amen.

Day Twenty-Nine

Living Abundantly Through Joy

Joy and peace are closely associated to most people. In today's society, joy is the highest level of happiness. You can be happy, but extreme happiness is joy. However, that is not biblical. Like peace, you can always have joy because joy comes from God. Happiness is temporary and based on circumstances; joy is not.

Joy is "a cheerful, calm delight in all the circumstances of life." You may wonder how that is possible when bad news comes. How can you be cheerful, calm, or delighted when you get a diagnosis, someone you love dies, your kids are sick, a marriage falls apart, etc.? It just doesn't make sense, does it?

First, you must remember that God is in control. Nothing happens outside of His will or knowledge. Trusting that He knows what you need and when you need it should bring comfort. Nothing you face takes your Heavenly Father by surprise. "For my thoughts are not your thoughts, neither are your ways my ways, saith the Lord. For as the heavens are higher than the earth, so are my ways higher than

your ways, and my thoughts than your thoughts."
Isaiah 55:8-9

"And the Lord, he it is that doth go before thee; he will be with thee, he will not fail thee, neither forsake thee: fear not, neither be dismayed."
Deuteronomy 31:8

Second, you must live by faith. Living a life of faith is trusting and believing God. When you trust and believe God, you take Him at His Word. This helps you to choose joy. Verses like Romans 8:28 bring comfort. "And we know that all things work together for good to them that love God, to them who are called according to his purpose." Everything you face has a purpose. There are no useless trials. James 1:2-4 says, "My brethren, count it all joy when ye fall into divers temptations; Knowing this, that the trying of your faith worketh patience. But let patience have her perfect work, that ye may be perfect and entire, wanting nothing." This passage assures you that you can choose joy in trials and that trials have a purpose; they strengthen and mature you.

Joy is possible because your confidence and assurance are based on God. You know He loves and cares for you. He is faithful, can be trusted, and knows what is best for you. Focusing on Christ takes your focus off of yourself, the trials, and the unknowns and places it on what you do know. This is why your personal Bible reading, study, and prayer times are vital to everyday life. You can't trust Someone you don't know. When you know God, you'll be able to trust Him.

Sin will always steal your joy. God will not let His children have joy and sin both. Spiritual warfare will also take your joy. You cannot do much to prevent this one from coming, but you can be proactive. Stay in prayer and keep your mind focused on the Lord. Spiritual warfare is not sin. But it can lead you to sin if you do not react correctly. Recognize the attack for what it is, and do not let your mind wander to a place of fear or bitterness. Keep Philippians 4:8 close and filter your thoughts through this verse. "Finally, brethren, whatsoever things are true, whatsoever things are honest, whatsoever things are just, whatsoever things are pure, whatsoever things are lovely, whatsoever things are of good report; if there be any virtue, and if there be any praise, think on these things." You need joy because it is your strength (Nehemiah 8:10), and strength is crucial to enduring spiritual warfare.

Dear Jesus,
Thank You for giving me joy in any circumstance. I know trials will come, and my joy will be tested. Please help me to look at You. I want to grow closer to You, trust You, and have the joy of the Lord in all situations. I pray that I will not trade my joy for temporary sinful pleasures. Thank You, Lord, for loving me and giving me this joy that comes from You. In Christ's name, I pray, Amen.

Day Thirty

Living Abundantly Through Goodness

"But the fruit of the Spirit is love, joy, peace, longsuffering, gentleness, goodness, faith," Galatians 5:22

"Surely goodness and mercy shall follow me all the days of my life: and I will dwell in the house of the Lord for ever." Psalm 23:6

"Oh how great is thy goodness, which thou hast laid up for them that fear thee; which thou hast wrought for them that trust in thee before the sons of men!" Psalm 31:19

"I had fainted, unless I had believed to see the goodness of the Lord in the land of the living." Psalm 27:13

Goodness is similar to charity in that it is action. Steven Currington's definition in his book, "Nevertheless I Live," says that goodness is "conforming our lives and conversations to behave benevolently toward others."

Think of what the word "conforming" means. Webster's 1828 dictionary defines conform as "Made to resemble, assuming the same form; like; resembling."

Isn't that what the Christian life is– conforming to be more like Christ and less like your sinful nature?

"And be not conformed to this world: but be ye transformed by the renewing of your mind, that ye may prove what is that good, and acceptable, and perfect, will of God." Romans 12:2

"That I may know him, and the power of his resurrection, and the fellowship of his sufferings, being made conformable unto his death;" Philippians 3:10

"And we know that all things work together for good to them that love God, to them who are the called according to his purpose. For whom he did foreknow, he also did predestinate to be conformed to the image of his Son, that he might be the firstborn among many brethren." Romans 8:28-29

Seek to be more like Christ so you can show this goodness to others. When you choose the opposite of goodness, this does not reflect Christ to others. Your flesh may want to choose meanness out of selfishness and pride. Meanness is "Unkindness, spitefulness, or unfairness." When you remember the goodness God has shown you, you can easily show goodness to others. It is easy to focus on the sin of others and say that they do not deserve goodness, but do not forget that God could rightly do the same to you! What a mess that would be! God's goodness in your life is based on Who He is, not what you have done. Just like His love, mercy, grace, and salvation, goodness is also unmerited.

A heart of love and a Spirit-led life will produce the outer work of goodness toward others. Choose to obey the Lord in this area. Especially when it is hard and you feel the recipient is undeserving. God loves those that seem undeserving just as much as He loves you or anyone else. Do not withhold showing goodness to someone. Choosing meanness will never bring someone to Christ.

Dear Lord,
Thank You for Your goodness to me! I do not deserve the kindness or the good gifts You have blessed me with. Lord, may I not have a heart or attitude of meanness toward anyone. Help me have a heart of love and a lifestyle of goodness. May the way I treat others be a clear reflection of You.
In Jesus' name,
Amen.

Day Thirty-One

Living Abundantly Through Temperance

"But the fruit of the Spirit is love, joy, peace, longsuffering, gentleness, goodness, faith, Meekness, temperance: against such there is no law." Galatians 5:22-23

"And beside this, giving all diligence, add to your faith virtue; and to virtue knowledge; And to knowledge temperance; and to temperance patience; and to patience godliness; And to godliness brotherly kindness; and to brotherly kindness charity. For if these things be in you, and abound, they make you that ye shall neither be barren nor unfruitful in the knowledge of our Lord Jesus Christ. But he that lacketh these things is blind, and cannot see afar off, and hath forgotten that he was purged from his old sins." 2 Peter 1:5-9

Temperance is defined as "Moderation, particularly habitual moderation in regard to the indulgence of the natural appetites and passions; restrained or moderate indulgence; as temperance in eating and drinking;"

It is possible to have too much of even good things. God wants you to have a balanced life. Going to an amusement park is not a sin, but going seven days per week every week and never taking care of other responsibilities is not being temperate with your time at the amusement park. Serving at church for 80 hours per week also is not having temperance. God still wants you to take care of your responsibilities at home and work, and He wants you to rest. It is easy to understand that sin is sin and not to entertain or indulge in that. Remember that there must also be temperance in good things. Temperance makes the rest of the fruit possible in your life. Without it, you will not be led by the Spirit. The opposite of temperance is self-indulgence. I dislike songs or Bible translations that change temperance to "self-control." You aren't to be self-controlled but Spirit-controlled in all life's pleasures. God is not against fun. He is against those things taking over your life.

When you are Spirit-controlled, you will live a moderate and balanced life. Remember that your pride and the Devil want to take good things, turn them into idols, and cause you to overindulge in good things.

Take your habits to the Lord and ask Him to show you if anything is out of balance. If He reveals anything to you, please trust and surrender that thing to Him. There is nothing more important than being right with God and others. Any habits or pleasures not done in moderation can negatively affect your physical, emotional, mental, and spiritual health and relationships with friends and family. When you surrender these things to the Lord and let go of things, you may feel less stressed. Habits and hobbies can take up so much time and put added pressure on yourself that you don't realize until you let them go. Remember, trusting God is always worth it.

Dear Lord,
Thank You for caring about what I allow into my life. I don't want to allow anything that hinders my relationship with You or others. Father, please show me anything I need to be more temperate with and help me find a healthy balance. I want to live a Spirit-led life, not a self-led life. Thank You for Your love for me and Your leadership in my life.
In Jesus' name,
Amen.

Thank you for taking the time to read this book! I pray it was a help and encouragement to you, and as a result, you will begin to live abundantly.

More from me: "Is Your Marriage a Priority?" is available on Amazon in paperback and Kindle.

Connect with me on Instagram @Proverbs_31life and my blog at www.inthemidst.home.blog.